Toronto
Then & Now

The Duff Homestead — Elm Grove Avenue — 1877

Toronto
Then & Now

J. Clarence Duff
with Sarah Yates

Fitzhenry & Whiteside

Fitzhenry & Whiteside Limited
Markham, Ontario

Editing: Frank English
Design: David Shaw

Sketches reproduced by permission of Cairn Capital Inc.

Canadian Cataloguing in Publication Data

Duff, J. Clarence (James Clarence), 1893-
   Toronto then and now

Bibliography: p.
ISBN 0-88902-950-4

1. Toronto (Ont.) - History.   2. Toronto (Ont.) — Description.   I. Title.

FC3097.4.D83 1983   971.35'41   C84-098011-6
F1059.5.T6857D83 1983

Printed and bound in Canada by John Deyell Company

Contents

List of Illustrations

Foreword

Those of us who have been around over eighty or ninety years have witnessed the tremendous expansion in the City of Toronto, particularly if we have been involved in her management.

I have known Clarence Duff for over seventy years. We both attended the Howard Park United Church as youngsters and from her choir we acquired our wives. We both made excellent choices.

We both put our shoulders to the work of progress because we believed in Toronto. We worked hard to develop her as a great city, each in his own way.

Clarence applied himself faithfully to his insurance business and, as a hobby, he applied himself to drawing his own pen-and-ink sketches of old Toronto for his annual calendar. These have filled one's archives with authentic proof of the past, for which everyone is gratified.

Frederick Gardiner

Lake Shore Road — Toronto-Long Branch-Port Credit Radial — 1900

Preface

The Creator made this part of the North American continent an abundantly productive area. Our ancestors were brave enough and wise enough to venture here and seek out their future in the unknown vastness, in search of what they did not have. They consisted mostly of Europeans, primarily from the British Isles, France and Spain. The Spanish tended toward the subtropical parts. Next came the mid-Europeans to the more temperate section.

The Dutch, French and British took to the more rugged and colder climates in the northern section of the continent. The British, being more hardy, made a firmer stand and outlasted all other nations and established the British language and law over most of the North American continent under which we benefited greatly. My grandparents and parents and the majority of the first settlers in Toronto were of this stock. My contention is that the geography and productivity of Toronto is a testament to man's ability to develop and harvest the abundant good of the land through the efforts of her hard-working people.

Shortly after the formation of the City of Toronto in 1834, a group of dedicated citizens decided to create the University of Toronto complete with its main building for the liberal arts and other departments of law, medicine and practical science (later named engineering). The University of Toronto and the School of Practical Science poured out thousands of graduates to make this beautiful city of ours one of the greatest educational centres of North America; and now, with the addition of York University, Ryerson and all the other community and technical colleges such as Seneca and George Brown, this prominence extends world wide. Therefore, I submit that our greatness emanates from the combination of our culture and our capacity in developing these fine institutions which nurture our abilities to learn and grow.

I had the good fortune of being born in Toronto. Some of the earlier inhabitants whose brilliance contributed greatly to the city, even as I was born here ninety years ago, included Egerton Ryerson, Dr. Henry Scadding and others who formulated good educational requirements giving Toronto a real lead in schooling and religious standards. It was a splendid start.

My scholastic efforts were not too rewarding. I did not like book learning, but I was inquisitive and creative and blessed with a photographic mind which filed away hundreds of early incidents and facts for future reference.

My father died early in my life and actually was buried on my sixth birthday in 1899. I never had much of Father's attention because he was in poor health all of those years. To learn what I missed, I studied all of my seniors, particularly men, pretty carefully and learned early to emulate those I admired. In my Sunday school and church days there were active and useful men around me — a large commercial hardware merchant, a gravestone maker, a builder, a slaughterhouse owner and a baker. Busy men were the active leading men. The same thing applied to the top men in the YMCA. I had occasion to rub shoulders with some of the biggest retail merchants, the president of the Consumers' Gas Company, the owner of a large appliance manu-facturing company and the owner of a wholesale grocery store which became one of Canada's giants. These men made a strong impression on me.

But my impressions, even my memory, were based on a person's values rather than the wages made by that person. It wasn't simply a man's bank account that interested or attracted me to him. Not that I did not enjoy my wages, but I did not admire excess profit or greed that appeared so often among those striving to get ahead in this world. I had a happy, satisfying life without that.

Consequently, my creation on the history of Toronto in the last ninety years has a different approach. My story embodies accounts of plenty of strong, capable and generous people as well as comments on the builders of things and what they built.

J. Clarence Duff

Toronto to the Junction — 1895

Arc-lamp lighter — North Lisgar Street and McKenzie Crescent — 1900

Sunnyside Level-crossing — 1889

Ontario Government House — King and Simcoe Streets — 1862-1912

Robert Simpson's Store — 184 Yonge Street — 1872

The "Mail" Building —
King and Bay Streets —
1881-1939

Crystal Palace — Industrial Exhibition Grounds — 1879-1906

Wellington, Church and Front Streets — 1863

CHAPTER ONE

The Early Years

In 1793 Governor Simcoe and his wife, Elizabeth, first came to York via a boat navigated by Jean Rousseau, descendant of a fur-trading family who had been in the area for one hundred years. They arrived on May 2, 1793, just one hundred years before I was born in the City of Toronto.

Just six years before this, in 1787, Lord Dorchester, the first Governor General of Canada, had negotiated the purchase of certain lands on the east and west sides of the Humber River. Three chiefs of the Mississauga Indians, acknowledged as owners of the land, made the deal. The Deputy Surveyor-General, John Collins, acted for the Crown. The price paid was seventeen hundred pounds of English money and much merchandise — barrels of cloth, axes and odds and ends, generally acknowledged as "dear to the heart of the simple savage". After the completion of the deal, all purchase papers relating to York property could be considered legal. Prior to this, those few individuals who had built on the land could not be given any legal deed to the property.

When Governor Simcoe and his wife came to York, they settled in a hastily erected tent on the site of their land, still today called Castle Frank after their son. The property was on a prominent knoll on the west bank of the Don Valley with a view down toward Lake Ontario. The Governor had a good view of the harbour in case of attack from the new Republic of America to its south.

He was particularly interested in the land survey which established the street plan for the townsite and later expansion of the city itself. He and his deputy-surveyor, Alexander Aitkin, laid out a grid of concession roads, one and one quarter miles apart, creating park lots for those soldiers and others who were to be ceded land in the newly established town. The entire area was then ten blocks bounded by George, Duke, Berkeley and Front streets with the Don River to the east. Yonge Street formed the north and south coordinate, and Queen Street, then known as Lot Street, was the east-west coordinate of the grid. These concession roads remain the basis of downtown Toronto today. Roads which stop suddenly and start again are most often the result of the many ravines, valleys, rivers, creeks and other natural geographical features of the land on which Toronto was settled.

In 1834 the City of Toronto was incorporated. The population was listed at 9254.

In 1891 our family lived in the west end of the city at 179 Perth Avenue. Bell Canada records from the time list our phone number as 5318. I was born with good eyes and have lived since that time to witness many thousands of changes in the daily life of the people, in the growth of the city and its skyline. Parents and grandparents, aunts and other relatives and friends have told me their stories. I have listened and remembered. This is my telling of the history of Toronto compiled from tales told to me and from things I have seen and experienced during my ninety years spent in this beautiful city. The changes in ideas, methods and the creation and invention of things was enormous. Many hard-working men and women, including our family, helped lay the foundation for this city's growth and progress.

Sir Sandford Fleming was one of these men. A Scottish immigrant from Greenwich, Scotland, Fleming came out to Canada in 1843 on the same ship as my Grandfather Duff. Fleming was a construc-tion engineer and in his new country he set up his own business and got a contract to build the Dundas Highway. He took my grandfather into the firm as an assistant.

Several years later my grandmother, Cecilia Eason, sailed from Glasgow with her parents to meet her husband-to-be, my grandfather, in Quebec. They were married on New Year's Eve that year, 1847, and Sandford Fleming was the best man at the ceremony.

Fleming contributed enormously to Toronto and to the world when he developed the concept of stan-dard time. Until this concept was established, world time was uncoordinated and chaotic. To arrive at the concept Fleming counted the meridians around the world and then allotted the time between meridians by dividing the circle of time by the time spent in one revolution of the earth. So, the earth was divided into twenty-four time zones, each separated by meridians fifteen degrees apart. Greenwich, England, was chosen as the starting point for the standard measurement. Fleming developed his concept in Toronto in November 1883 and released the information to the world in February 1884. After international meetings held in Russia, Italy and finally Washington, D.C., the idea was accepted world wide.

Queen Victoria knighted Sandford Fleming for his brilliant work. In 1938 a pillar was erected in front of the Sir Sandford Fleming Laboratory on the University of Toronto grounds to commemorate him.

I was born on the twenty-sixth day of July 1893. The house where I was born was on the east side of Perth Avenue. The lot was fenced with a white picket fence across the front and down the sides to the back verandah with a wire fence to close in the back yard. The wire fence had heavy posts and our mastiff, Prince, was chained to one of these. We needed him, because it was some years before our street was lighted and my father was not a rugged man.

Inside the front yard from the fence to the house was a large flower bed of roses and many other varieties of flowers. Against the white-painted house and fence were red climbing roses. Down the side of the house was a row of currant bushes. There was a large pear tree by the back steps. A stout slat side-walk led to the rear of the yard, and behind a hedge of strong dahlias was a two-holer for the convenience of the family.

Inside the house each room had a washstand and in the cupboard a chamber pot for the nightly relief of the family member and for convenience in the cold weather. This article was called the thunder mug. Two years later, the sewers were laid on our street and we installed the overhead box and pull chain.

Our street was a sand road with wooden curbs. There was not enough horse-drawn traffic on it even to supply fertilizer for our garden, so for this purpose I was sent regularly to the Puddy Brother's Slaughter-house across the railway tracks for two small pails of blood to mix with the light soil. The garden was my visual classroom where I always got good marks and green thumbs. I liked assisting Father in the garden as a young boy and it put me in good stead all through my later life.

From our house we looked out the front door through one hundred and eighty yards of corn to the trains, the Grand Trunk and the Gray and Bruce Lines. Their officials had been approached by Mr. Carpmael, Director of the Meteorological Division in Toronto, with a proposal for an ingenious method of weather broadcasting.

A banner was attached to the side of the express train on every train out of Toronto with information giving the latest weather forecast. The forecast could then be used to guide the day's operations. The code consisted of a full moon to indicate fine weather; a crescent moon to indicate showers and a star to indicate thunderstorms and rain. Every morning we and hundreds of Ontario farmers checked the passing trains for the weather forecast.

From Dundas Street west, Bloor Street was then just a sand road, up and down hill, flanked by verdant land full of bushes. Spring offered us many natural phenomena to observe there. The warmth of the water in the swamp soon energized insect eggs to life. The most notable sight was the dragonfly beetles which climbed up the stalks of the rushes, hooked their claws onto the stalk and let the sun do the rest. As the heat dried the beatle's shell, it cracked open. The bulging eyes of the dragonfly's head appeared first. Slowly, the body and legs were exposed. Then the long, slim body uncurled until it extended straight out behind. In a couple of hours, if the sun was hot, the wings which had unfolded, would start to flutter. This was awfully interesting. After a short while, if you took your eyes away and

then turned back, the dragonfly was gone. I have watched this emergence many times. While waiting and watching and listening you heard the call of the spring birds — the song sparrow, the red-winged blackbird, the robin, finch, bluejay, oriole, and a number of warblers.

Before the hollow on Bloor Street was filled up, it used to be quite an adventure to walk out Bloor to the Humber River. Swansea, south of Bloor and west of Grenadier Pond, had been a thriving town just before this period and the Swansea Bolt Works was the major place of employment.

To the northeast of their plant was the big marsh or swamp where we kids used to hunt frogs and garter snakes. One of the things I remember was the exhaust valve of the steam boiler sounding when the Bolt Works was in operation. It would blow every few moments with the kind of snort that I imagined a rhinoceros would make.

In the summer, Mother would send us out on berry-picking expeditions. I was the youngest of the pickers. She would pack us a lunch and we were to pick until twelve o'clock noon, not eating our lunch until then. The bushes were full of all sorts of berries in season — strawberries, raspberries, blueberries and huckleberries — and we picked them all. Mother would use all of these berries together to make her own special mixture. She called it Bloor Street jam, a family favourite for years.

While picking berries, I used my inquisitiveness well. I loved the outdoors and my garden training at home made me observant of all that went on around me in nature. One of the earliest of the lovely wild flowers, which I noticed on our jaunts, was the trailing arbutus. It could be found in the warm sands of the flatlands in the northern part of High Park.

21

Slattery's Grove and Hotel "The Pines" — Dundas and Bloor Streets — 1877

The little bell of a flower was about the size of a lily-of-the-valley and quite as fragrant, but with fewer blooms on the small creeper. I guess God wanted the squirrel, chipmunk and grasshopper to enjoy breathing while scampering over the soil. I never could understand why it was so rare. The lupin blossomed in the same area about a month later. Today, the lupin has been cultivated and is grown in many Toronto gardens.

The next most interesting flower was the hepatica, a delicate pink-to-purple coloured flower on two- to three-inch furry stems. These grew in clumps of from eight to thirty and had a very delicate, sweet perfume. The hepatica was easily transplanted for domestic use. Then, of course, there were the violets and trilliums, swamp marigolds and skunk cabbages.

Slattery's Hotel on the southwest corner of Dundas and Bloor streets was famous as the place for the annual Thanksgiving fox hunt of the Toronto Hunt Club.

The day would be one of great excitement — the traditional pomp and ceremony of the hunt itself; the high-pitched sound of the foxhorn; the sleek coats of the horses, brushed to perfection; the bright red jackets of the hunters and the yelping dogs. They would leave the premises on Bloor and ride through the Humber Valley on the chase.

The day would have been crisp, cold and clear, the hunt successful and the club members would gather back at the hotel for an evening's entertainment. Spirits were high. A sumptuous dinner was provided and the innkeeper had lined up an evening of cock fights for entertainment to follow. The loft above the riding shed was packed and smoky; the fights fierce. With his supply of cocks depleted, however, his guests were still spoiling for more fun and the innkeeper needed another fighter. He knew where to find one.

For some months past, our dog, Prince, had been a regular at the Slattery's Hotel where he could count on receiving a hearty bone from the hotel's dining room remains. So when the cocks were all spent, Prince was brought into the ring with the neighbouring farmer's billygoat. Although the two were unlikely opponents in the ring and good friends out of it, teasing from the onlookers soon made them fight. It was a butting, biting, lunging match that ensued, with Prince finally declared the winner. They were pulled apart before any real damage was done. Even so, that week Prince suffered bruised ribs and disgrace at home. He wasn't allowed outside without somebody watching over him. We weren't keen to have him suffer a repeat performance.

One of my duties was to watch for the milkman. Milk, bread, farm produce and other staples were then peddled door to door along the dusty streets. We could hear the familiar cowbell before the milkman would come into sight. He had a slow, plodding horse pulling a light buckboard, and a box on it for a seat and behind that two cans of milk. In one can was a long dipstick with a pint measure on the end. We would take a large pitcher or two out to the cart to be filled; the charge, I think, was about four cents a quart.

The kindly gentleman was none other than William Neilson, of Neilson chocolate fame. The Neilson family all got into merchandising early. The boys, Charles, Allen and Morden, drove out into the country in the early morning for the milk; Mr. Neilson drove the milk cart around the city streets; and Mrs. Neilson ran a cake store at Lynd Avenue

Street Sprinkler — 1900

and Dundas Street West. The cream from the milk that was left over daily was turned into fine icing for the excellent cakes which Mrs. Neilson baked. Later, Neilson's also became famous for ice cream and when ice cream sales dropped, Mr. Neilson invented the Eskimo pie and made chocolate and even cocoa. In the 1920s their ice cream was so popular that it was served on all the luxury liners crossing the Atlantic between Canada and England.

Ice for the old iceboxes was cut from Lake Simcoe or manufactured in two ice-manufacturing plants. Two ice delivery companies, the Belle Ewart and the Lake Simcoe, delivered ice on our street at the turn of the century. Heavy, red, covered wagons with yellow lettering on the side were loaded down with forty-pound blocks to be cut in half and then in half again to ten-pound blocks to be carried inside and put into the icebox. It was a big summer business!

How the kids hung around when the driver was splitting the blocks! If he didn't put the chisel into the block exactly right, a couple of large chips of ice would be freed. They would fall to the bottom of the cart and spill onto the road. On a hot summer day they would be tops, a real find for one of us children. We would run with the chip to the tap, wash it off and then slurp the cold ice until it was gone.

The street sprinkler provided another summer-time frolic for us kids. The water container was a half cistern painted blue, with four white-painted iron rings holding it together, mounted on two big axles with a sprinkler tube across the rear out of which spouted the water. The driver sat on top of the tank with a lever that turned the spray on and off. When the tank ran dry, he pulled up at the nearest hydrant, connected a hose to the hydrant and filled up again. He would ride around street after street to wash down the mud and dust and to cool down the area on hot summer days. When he did our street, we tried to get in the spray and catch all the water we could.

The city had been wired for electricity in 1889 and in 1890 many gas lights were dismantled to make way for electric street lighting. Down in the centre of the city, however, were rows of beautiful gas lamps. Our area, when it was finally lighted, was lit with arc lamps whose power was supplied by the Toronto Electric Company.

The arc lamp was suspended on a twenty-five foot pole on a steel bracket about eight feet out over the road. When the current was turned on, the upper carbon would slide down the rods by force of gravity and make the contact. The parts were encased in a large glass bowl and gave the splendid light that was characteristic of these lights. A rope passing through a couple of pulleys was used to raise and lower the lamp for the renewal of the carbon stems.

Every day the carbon stick was renewed by the lamplighter who drove a small cart with his supplies aboard. He also had to polish the bowl. His supplies included a glass-footed stool to act as insulation protection against the current. Mr. Bowen, the man who fixed the lamps on our street, was one of our neighbours. His son, Bert, was my constant chum. All the children on the street waited for the carbons to be changed because the burnt carbon stick was used by the girls to mark out the hopscotch areas on the sidewalk. The boys never competed with the girls because they were too awkward. To me, the girls' efforts were the preliminary manoeuvres of ballerinas.

This was Toronto in the 1890s, a city whose

population had expanded to about 200,000 people. In its growth, Toronto had already absorbed half a dozen neighbouring municipalities. The city contained many thriving businesses, elegant mansions with accompanying large properties and many less wealthy establishments such as the workingman's home in which we lived. Farmers still used Davenport Road, an old Indian trail, still dust-covered, to transport their goods for sale to the St. Lawrence Market. There was a tollgate at the top of Bathurst Street hill to collect money for the paving of this and other streets. The Dominion Bank had been established to offset the Bank of Montreal's power and to invest in the many Canadian projects of which the Bank of Montreal had become wary. It was still presided over by James Austin, owner of the Spadina estate, who also headed the Consumers' Gas Company which had been established by him and others in 1848.

The city had been wired for commercial purposes in 1889. The power lines carried heavy voltage and it was a good few years before domestic use was made possible. The first electricity for Toronto use emanated from the Toronto Electrical Company's steam plant, located just east of Yonge Street down on the bay front. The steam power plant used many hundreds of tons of coal. This was stockpiled in tremendous bins brought in by sailing ships and later by rail. Where water power was used to generate electricity, as in Niagara Falls, the burden for the steam plants was made much easier.

While the battle between gas and electricity raged, many outside gas lights were dismantled but inside lighting continued to use gas because the cost was half that of electricity. Between 1883 and 1893, the year that I was born, the amount of gas sold by

Consumers' Gas doubled and in the next ten-year span, it did the same again.

The first telephone service in Toronto was provided by the Toronto Telegraph Despatch Company. Then, in April 1880, Bell Canada was incorporated and it started to provide the service. In May 1901, Bell Telephone announced that because of the large number of telephones in use in Toronto, they would create three central offices from which calls could be routed. Up until then, there had been only one and the lines had been badly congested. The first three Toronto exchanges were Main with numbers from 1 to 4466; Park from 1 to 865 and North from 1 to 2125.

Thereafter, as the city grew and the number of telephones increased, more exchanges were added. The first telephones were cranked, not dialled, and connected to an operator. A light would go on in the exchange office, the operator would answer your call, ask what number you wanted and connect you. The first business phone in Toronto was in our present Royal York Hotel.

The Allan Gardens or Horticultural Gardens as they were sometimes called, located at the south-west corner of Carlton and Sherbourne streets, were considered one of Toronto's most beautiful establishments. The land, originally owned by the Honourable William Allan in 1803, had been donated to the citizens of Toronto for use as a park by his son in 1857.

The large glass pavilion known as the Palm House, built in 1879, was used for concerts, balls and promenades, conventions and flower shows. In 1895 the Royal Canadian Yacht Club held its annual meeting there.

Its daily promenades soon gained a reputation for

being one of Toronto's most notable events especially on a sunshiny day. It was here that the nannies and their charges from all the wealthy homes on Jarvis Street and neighbourhood met for their daily gossip. Word spread and the promenade became quite a show. All the girls would be dressed up in their best; bonnets would be colourful, gowns crisp and pretty and perambulators bedecked with umbrellas and all the other trimmings to show them at their fanciful best. Carriages were elegant and often elaborate, made with wicker, leather and cloth. Policemen in the area would make a point of catching the parade of neatly dressed nursemaids and their charges and more than one romance started there. I remember one aunt's stories of the girls' highjinks and high fashion. My older brothers no doubt also frequented the place, but I was too young.

The Palm Room contained many rare palms and plants, plus lots of beautiful flowers. Unfortunately, it was beleaguered with fires and had to be rebuilt a number of times. In 1902 it was finally burned to the ground; and in 1909 the present greenhouse was built to replace it.

As the city grew and prospered around us, my father's health began to fail. It became more and more difficult for him to travel the distance to his job as a clerk at Osgoode Hall. We moved several times, living on Sorauren Avenue and then finally to Cottingham Street, just east of Poplar Plains Road.

On the south side of Cottingham was the North Central Toronto Pumping Station. It was very quiet there until the fire alarm on the wall clanged. I spent many a happy hour there in the quiet and also in the confusion caused by the alarm.

What impressed me were the large ponderous wheels and big pistons on the pumps as well as the beautifully polished brass oil cups and fittings.

Sleighing was a favourite winter pastime which always got us into mischief. One winter's day, my brother Lou undertook to ride down Poplar Plains Road. It was a winding road and fairly steep. As he was coasting down, a cutter with a coachman driving came up the hill. The coachman luckily saw Lou and checked his horses. They reared just high enough for him to get under their legs safely and scoot down the rest of the way. Lou never tried to take that ride again. The incident was evidently reported because a police constable soon saw that the sleighing there was stopped completely.

Immediately to the left of Poplar Plains Road on the edge of the escarpment was the Nordheimer estate owned by the people of Nordheimer Piano fame. The first Mr. Nordheimer had done much to develop the musical tastes of Toronto when it was a much younger city.

A creek and dense bush cut across the road and the escarpment was populated with lovely homes — the estates of the Pellatts, the Austins, the Eatons and others in the succeeding years. The air was clean and quiet.

Religion played an important role in Toronto's early growth. Business, religion and influence frequently overlapped. Timothy Eaton was a young Irish youth who encompassed all three. As a young farm boy, he was brought up by his widowed mother who was a devout Presbyterian. He came to Kirkton, Ontario in 1857 and opened his first store there at the age of twenty-three. A couple of years later he joined his brother, James, in St. Marys where they opened a dry goods store.

Timothy married Margaret Beattie and six years

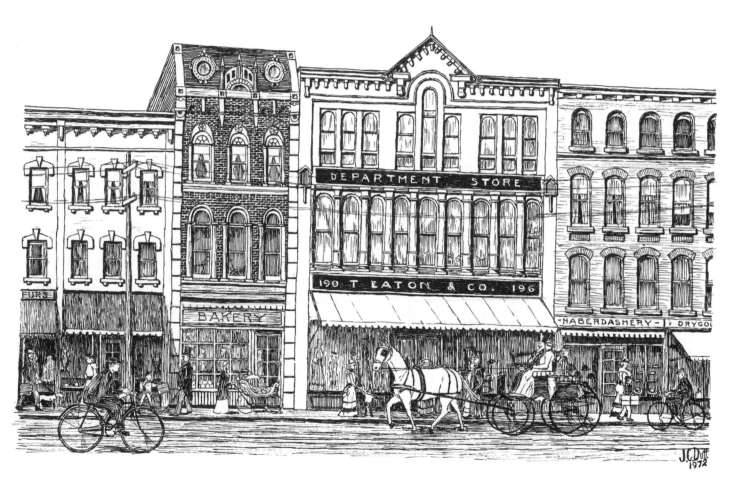

Eaton's — 190 Yonge Street — 1883

later he sold his interests in the shop at St. Marys. He invested the $6500 from it in a dry goods shop at 178 Yonge Street which had been owned by James Jennings. In 1873, the business had outgrown the premises at 178 so he bought a block of three stores further up Yonge Street, just north of Queen. He had the insides of the brick buildings gutted and converted into a three-storey shop with higher ceilings and the possibility for better merchandising display areas. It was called 190 Yonge Street. This was the beginning of the T. Eaton Empire.

Mr. Eaton practised Christianity at all times. He was an honest man and disliked the bartering type of business. So he instituted a new type of merchandising — selling for cash at one low price and promising the return of money to his customers for goods which were not satisfactory, a policy Eaton's still honours today.

All sales desks in the store were connected with the office by pneumatic tubes for carrying cash for the sale, and return change if any was necessary. Customers were served quickly, given a parcel, neatly wrapped and a courteous "thank you".

Mr. Eaton was kind and considerate to his employees. At Christmas time he would give a festive dinner for all of his staff and their families until there were over two thousand on his payroll and the undertaking became too immense.

Eaton's was one of the first stores in Toronto to put in elevators to the top floor of their building. It was necessary to carry dressed dummies up and down in them for some time to let the customers know that they were safe and were meant for passenger travel.

The Eaton's catalogues went everywhere in Canada. They helped the immigrant to learn English with the words printed under the pictures of the articles; they helped settlers in the west to choose furnishings for their homes. One Inuit wrote to order an afternoon frock and was disappointed when it arrived without the woman who had modelled it for the catalogue. His money was refunded when he complained, "Where's the woman?"

The fame of Eaton's store rose phenomenally because of Mr. Eaton's merchandising practices. He sold no liquor, tobacco nor playing cards because of his strict principles. Curtains closed off store display windows on Sundays.

A fine gentleman, Timothy Eaton, can today be remembered by the church donated to the United Church of Canada, free of any encumbrances, by his wife and family at the time of his death in 1907. The marvellous buildings are at 230 St. Clair Avenue West. They are still called the Timothy Eaton Memorial Church.

But for those of us still living in the latter part of the nineteenth century, life continued to be difficult. In our front parlour Rosamond, my sister, would play the tune "Narcissus" on the piano, again and again. It gave great pleasure to our Dad as he lay in the front bedroom overlooking a good-sized crabapple tree on the front lawn. It was the end of May and the tree was in full bloom. He died of what doctors called a rheumatic heart on July 21, 1899. The last solid memory I have of my father was when he took me to the barber shop to get my shoulder length curls cut off. Our two twin girls had come along and it was no longer necessary for me to parade as a girl. That day, we bought an extra Dutch brown loaf of bread from which I got the crusts at both ends. In a family with four boys always calling for the crusts, this was a treat!

Now, at Father's death, my Mother was left a widow with seven children, the oldest a girl of fourteen years, and with limited funds. The only ray of comfort came from the fact that Father had, very early in life, been persuaded to buy two thousand dollars' worth of life insurance. Very little insurance was bought in that era and two thousand dollars was considered to be a nice nest egg. Mother was fine and strong, a good organizer and a loving parent. Her first thought was to find somewhere for us to live.

The search for a house turned up a two-storey, brick-front, seven-room, plaster-sided, semi-detached house at 256 Lisgar Street, back in the west end. The house was bought for eighteen hundred dollars. Mother put one thousand dollars down which left us a mortgage of eight hundred dollars with which to do battle.

The other thousand dollars was put out to interest and the earnings on that went toward putting some food on the table. At our own family conference, Mother, our captain, told us what was expected of us. We all agreed to follow orders. Our first rule was to be the best family in the district — clean, neat and polite, friendly and respectful of all property. The boys had to do kitchen duty and the girls were in charge of the bedrooms and setting the table. One of us boys also had to cut the kindling and see that the scuttle was full of coal for the early morning fire. The stove had a hot-water coil in the front box to boil the kitchen and cooking water. Our rotation of duties changed each Sunday night.

The house had an earthen floor in the basement, and in the front half of the house, the basement was partitioned off around the furnace. Heat was kept out of the back portion in which we stored our winter's supply of food. A farmer by the name of Mr. Griffith made a regular call on us each fall bringing in bags of potatoes and barrels of apples and other vegetables. He was very kind and, seeing that we paid in cash, he was happy to serve us, charging a reasonable price for his merchandise.

The first thing we did on Lisgar Street to make ourselves known and wanted was to convert our henhouse into a clubhouse. This was done in quick order with the assistance of Grandpa Richey. Everything in the interior was torn out. The walls were whitewashed; a new floor was laid; and new tarpaper was put on the walls. A fireplace shelf was put up on the north wall under which I drew a fireplace in coloured chalk to make it more homey. Somebody found an old table with a pretty good top which was edged with stripping. Holes were drilled in the surface into which we fixed hoops; this made an excellent croquet table. We had a lot of fun on this creation as well as with dominoes, croquinole and other games.

All the neighbourhood boys were welcome once they had passed Mother's inspection. The two older brothers, Alex and Lou, looked out for us and supervised. They were already members of the west end YMCA located at Queen and Dovercourt.

Our curfew was darkness because there were no lights that might create a fire hazard. No girls were allowed. Any fighting was punished by removal from the club.

In winter we flooded the yard and played hockey. The snow that was shovelled off the hockey area was piled against the clubhouse between the fence and a tree, packed down hard and made into a mound down which we could slide using barrel staves for skis. It was a lot of fun. My brother Alex was one of the first skiers in the Toronto area and he later had a pair of skis sent over from Norway. However, this was not until 1912.

Mother was always one of the gang and helped where she could. One day there was a loose board over top of the door of the clubhouse and it bothered us. We climbed the ladder and tried, without success, to pry it free. So Mother grabbed the hammer, climbed the ladder herself and yanked the board free for us. However, as she pried it loose, she lost her balance and tipped over backward onto her head. Luckily for us, she landed in a flower pot and it was this and not her head which was broken.

Cash flow was of tremendous importance for us now. The boys were all going to school so time out of school was important. Alex contacted the newspaper offices and found that routes in our area were open for delivery boys. We promptly accepted the jobs. We were thirteen, twelve, nine and seven years of age. As the youngest, I got the route nearest home. We reported to a Mr. McLean who carted the papers — the *Globe*, the *Mail and Empire* and the *Morning World* — to the boys on Queen Street. Both the *Globe* and the *Mail and Empire* sold for two cents and the *Morning World* sold for one cent a copy.

Mr. McLean delivered his papers in an ordinary express wagon in bundles much like today's papers. He would arrive at the drop-off spot at 5 a.m. and we had to be there before then to meet him. He would give us the papers and the customer list with strict instructions before sending us on our way. We had to fold the papers and put them in the mailboxes or under the mats, not throw them on the verandahs or walks. If a customer complained, we were docked some of our pay.

My delivery route only lasted until a heavy snowstorm made walking on the streets difficult. I was too short; my bag dragged in the snow; and I became fagged. So, the older boys took over my route and set me up a selling station at the corner of Lisgar and Dundas streets. It was a streetcar stop and I worked up a good trade there over the years. I used to help two blind men onto the streetcar every morning. I traded newspapers with the local milkman in exchange for a small bottle of cream; I also traded with the Boyle and Libby Pop factory boss for a big bottle of cream soda or sarsaparilla for myself which I would take home.

I got to be very friendly with the conductors and in the summertime they would allow me to stand on the running boards of the open streetcars to sell my papers to the riders. Then one day I got careless and jumped off right in front of a horse pulling a cart. Some people took me into the drugstore and there a Mr. Godard offered to take me home in his chain-driven automobile truck. Thus, I probably had the first motorized ambulance ride in Toronto. It was 1902!

At this time the Dundas car turned south to Queen Street at what is now Ossington Avenue; the east-west street from Ossington to Bathurst was Arthur Street.

Besides handling paper routes, groceries, shovelling snow and cutting grass, we did any chores we could find. A silver mug was put on the shelf of the sideboard in the dining room and all our earnings were put into the mug and the money was used for food.

In the winter, sleighing at High Park was a favourite pastime. We would go as a gang of the four boys from the family, the three sisters, friends and sometimes even Mother. So, Grandpa Richey decided to build a suitable bobsleigh for us. He secured a ten-foot plank, made two sleighs as a base, reinforced them, put steel runners on them and reinforced the sleigh frame to accept a plate or t-bar as a steering post. A lever brake was attached to the rear sleigh to allow us to slow down or to help turn us around. There was a rounded wooden bar on either side of the plank, and the passengers held onto these. It was the finest of its kind in Toronto.

Before the bobsleigh was finished, we had searched the park from end to end to find the best place to use it. This location happened to be on the slope to the north of caretaker Lightfoot's home and down the hill to Grenadier Pond. There was one difficulty: an old board fence halfway down the hill which had partially fallen down. We decided that a gentle shove would tumble the rest of the fence, clearing the way for us. A staunch friend of Alex, Sam Vogan, whose parents ran a confectionery store on the corner of Brookfield and Queen, joined in this venture with enthusiasm. We inaugurated the High Park Slides in this venture. In later years, one track for the bobsleighs and two for the toboggans were operated by the Parks Department of Toronto. They gave good clean fun to thousands of Torontonians.

In our earlier days we had to haul the heavy bobsleigh to the Park and then back to our Lisgar Street house whenever we were finished the run. At a later date, the city provided a storage shed for the use of bobsleighers, and for a fee you could leave your sleigh there during the week.

The road to the east end of the slides ran down past the animal pens. It was also put into service as a bobsleigh route and traffic was banned from it. This made an excellent fast ride.

Grandpa Richey made himself a sleigh about three feet wide on which we rode out to Lorne Park in the winter. We would stop at Featherstonehaugh's for a drink for the horse. It was halfway there. Reaching the park, we would light a fire, make ourselves a cup of tea and then return home.

At Christmas time, or on other rare occasions, our Uncle Frank would send a Victoria Coach or a sleigh with a pair of horses and a coachman to take us down to the Richey household for Christmas dinner and a tree. Uncle Frank, Mother's brother, owned a livery stable next door to where they lived at 964 Queen Street West. His place was called the Golden's Livery.

If the weather was fair, the top would be down and we would have plenty of buffalo robes to pile on top of us. The coachman wore a plug hat. This would make for good gossip behind the neighbours' curtains, but for us it was a happy day which started early at home with our own tree.

Parlour games were popular at Christmas time. Carpet ball was an indoor variety of lawn bowling which our family enjoyed. It was played more gently, with coloured china balls, and preferably indoors with a long stretch of hall. The Richey grandparents' home was ideal since it had over thirty feet of hall between front door and kitchen door. Grandpa Richey was an active carpenter, a rugged builder; and he often joined in to play with us. After the game was over, we held a family singsong around the piano. All our family loved that singing.

When dinner was over, Grandma Richey would be escorted from the dining room to the living room where her rocking chair would sit beside the triangular black box of the grand piano. With a crocheted bonnet on her head, she sat there in all her glory, smiling benignly. She was sixty-five.

The City of Toronto had continued to grow and prosper and as the nineteenth century had come to an end, they had decided to mark their success by commissioning a new City Hall. In 1891, architect E.J. Lennox had won the competition for the design. He was one of the city's most prominent architects of the time and had given us the Bloor Street United Church, the King Edward Hotel, Massey Hall and, later, Casa Loma.

There were many battles at City Council over the building and many changes were made before the final job was finished for two and a half million dollars, two and a half times the original estimated figure. It was a beautiful building of Credit Valley brownstone and the city was rightfully proud. Every stone in the building was hand-tooled, and each layer of stones had a different thickness. The stone medallions and cornices and square windows were also handcut. The multiple swag of peaked roofs gave the whole building a solid geometrical appearance. It was an architectural marvel with a magnificent three-hundred-foot tower with carved stone gargoyles extending eight feet out below the clock. These stone gargoyles were eventually removed because erosion caused by the extreme climatic changes made them a hazard.

The inside of the building matched the beauty of the exterior. The colourful mosaic floors were laid by Italian artisans. There was a fifteen-foot marble main staircase with beautiful ornamental iron banisters. Everywhere you looked, beauty and strength blended to create respect and the feeling of power.

At the time of its building, the large clock at the top of the tower was the largest hand-wound clock in North America with massive bells to mark the progress of time. The quarter-hour bell weighed eighteen hundred and five pounds, the half-hour bell weighed thirty-three hundred and forty pounds and the hour bell weighed eleven thousand, six hundred and eighty-four pounds.

Toronto was justly proud of its accomplishments and the new City Hall seemed to mark its proud progress into the new century. However, by the last day of the century, December 31, 1899, the machinery to ring the bells had not come. The mayor of the day, the Honourable John Shaw, was not easily daunted by this circumstance. He took his councillors to the top of the tower, had them stuff their ears with cotton and swing the sledgehammers manually against the bells to ring in the twentieth century.

But a city's progress does not continue without serious setbacks and disasters. On April 19, 1904, my brother Cecil and I had been out together delivering a message. We were on our way home when we saw smoke over a factory we knew as the Newcombe Piano Factory. It looked to us to be the source of all the billowing smoke. It was a cold April day; the thermometer registered at 24 degrees Fahrenheit; and there was a thirty-mile-an-hour northwest wind. We were not dressed heavily enough to take the cold so we decided to run home and put on something warmer before exploring the fire. That was our first big mistake!

When we walked in the front door out of breath, Mother greeted us with relief, "Am I glad you're home," she exclaimed. "And now you must stay. Your aunt has just called to tell me about the terrible fire that is raging downtown!"

So we missed that awful night of excitement. My Aunt Elizabeth, mother's sister, was the secretary-treasurer of the firm, The Toronto Hamilton Sewer

Trolley Car — 1893

Pipe Company. They had just managed to salvage their books from the office before it was completely destroyed by fire. She happened to be working in the building only two away from the E. and S. Currie Building where the fire started and she saw it all.

From tales she told us and from the newspaper accounts of the day, we learned the news. The first alarm had been sent in from Box Number Twelve at 8:04 p.m. from King and Bay streets. At 8:30 p.m. with the fire spreading, a second alarm was sent out as warning. By 9:00 p.m. there was a general alarm. Every able body on the fire department's force was involved — one hundred and ninety-six men, thirty-six pieces of equipment from fifteen firehalls and twenty-six suburban stations with all their men and equipment. The call for assistance also went out to Hamilton, London, Brantford and Niagara Falls. Buffalo answered the calls for help with thirty men and two fire engines, arriving on a special train with open track clearance, and a cheer went up from the crowd. Our men had become exhausted.

Water pressure of seventy-five to seventy-eight pounds per square inch was not sufficient to the task. My aunt reported that the roar of the updraft was deafening and the sight of the fire spectacular. It was like an inferno fanned by the fierce wind. The intense heat doubled the force of the wind, and to add to the noise each fire engine had a special horn to call for more fuel to keep steam up in their pumps. The amazing thing was that the horses did not act nervous. They didn't move unless requested to do so by their drivers.

The spectacular sight of the buildings burning on both sides of the street seemed to be a vault or arch from which burning embers were scattered in showers.

As the perimeter of the fire spread, the firemen could not fight the interior. All they could do was try to control the edges. At one point the army was asked if they could supply sappers and dynamite to level the buildings in the path of the fire. The army didn't have the dynamite so they offered a unit with armoured guns and shells to destroy the foundations. This was refused.

The fire was stopped on its westward charge by the staff of the Queen's Hotel on Front Street. The staff hung out blankets and kept them wet on all eastern exposures until the danger was past. The *Telegram* and its staff did the same thing on the fire's northern charge up Bay Street. The Customs Building at Front Street and Yonge was also a big assistance to the firemen since its west wall was a perfect fire wall with no openings of any kind nor anything through which the fire could take a hold. There was a vacant lot on the west side of the building.

Despite the fire department's valiant efforts, ninety buildings and their contents were destroyed, and five thousand employees were idled with no immediate chance of recovery. The building loss was estimated at ten million dollars. Uninsured losses were staggering. The insurance covered only the direct loss of most buildings and contents if separately insured, but the time lost in production and profits through the damage done by the fire was not covered. There were no unemployment benefits to act as insurance for families of workers thrown out of work nor compensation for the owners. The kindness of the neighbours and savings accounts at the bank were the only cushion, because there was not any organized welfare in the city. Not since the great King Street Fire in April 1849 when the city lost its old Town Hall, the Market Place and St. James' Cathedral had the city been so devastated by fire.

It surely was a wonderful thing that there were no fatalities and so few injuries suffered in the holocaust. The Fire Chief got a sprained ankle early in the fire when he and four other men were trapped on the fifth floor of a building and had to slide to safety down a hose tied to the roof. The chief, the last man down, lost his grip when the hose slipped and fell the final distance to the ground.

One hundred and fifty established businesses were destroyed that night.

Queen's Wharf — Western Gap — 1895

Tinning's Wharf — Foot of York Street — 1836

Privat's Hotel — On sandbar in Toronto Bay — 1851-1858

Niagara Navigation Company Steamer *Chicora* — Yonge Street Wharf — 1890

Toronto Waterfront looking east from Simcoe Street — 1894

J.C.Duff.
1938

Great Western Railway Station — Yonge and Esplanade Streets — 1896

An early drawing by the author
at the age of 11 years, probably copied
from a nineteenth-century illustration

Foot of Yonge Street — 1900

CHAPTER TWO

The Social Years

Toronto's harbour has played a crucial role in her history. Ten years before Simcoe's arrival, the first survey of Lake Ontario harbours had been made and mention had been made of Toronto Bay, as it was then known.

Governor Simcoe noted the harbour's importance and recommended that it be used by the British fleet for defence purposes. Her location made her easily defensible and her distance from the American shore made her a safer harbour in which to keep British warships than the Kingston harbour then in use.

On his arrival, Simcoe erected a fort on the west bank of Garrison's Creek and had the first wharf built. It was 1793. A canal and sluices were built and the mouth of the creek was closed to facilitate loading and unloading of cargo.

Since that time, the harbour has changed its appearance greatly due to the natural forces of the wind and shifting sands of the bay and to man's efforts. I have always watched and loved the waterfront because it holds the key to so much of Toronto's past and her future.

Then, a peninsula of land jutted out from the marshy area currently known as Leslie Street, extending in a curve across to the tip of the sandbar closing in the eastern end of the harbour completely. The marshy area thus confined by the sandbar was impossible to navigate with any but the smallest of craft. Ships had to use the shallow fourteen-foot Western Gap to enter the harbour known as Toronto Bay.

No doubt the Indians had used the sandy beach along Toronto's natural shoreline as one of their trails before the arrival of the white man. Marshy and fertile, the home of thousands of birds and fish, it was the source of much food for the Indians as well as a natural avenue of transportation. The same reeds that made the harbour so fertile proved to be a great problem for early sailing vessels and frequent attempts were made to control them.

Soon after York was settled and trading increased, many privately owned wharves were built and much of the waterfront became privately owned and occupied. For forty years after Simcoe's arrival, there was no preservation of the harbour; nor were any improvements made. No control was exercised over its use. Many of the wharves were not maintained and fell into disrepair.

By the time the city was incorporated in 1834 and William Lyon Mackenzie had been made her first mayor, citizens were already concerned about their harbour. It was crucial for the shipment of all grain and other produce not grown in the settlement, an important source of commerce and communications. Funds were allocated by the city to improve and preserve the harbour. Another wharf that was built was called the King's Wharf, later the Queen's Wharf, which was publicly owned. (A replica of the lighthouse built in 1855 is now located on Lakeshore Boulevard between Tip Top Tailors and Loblaws where the original Queen's Wharf extended into the Western Gap.)

Regulations were made that all sunken wharves

were to be removed and that no ship was to discharge her ballast in the harbour. Most of the land along the waterfront up until that time was privately owned, and application was made by the city for patents to buy the remaining waterlots and the adjoining land to build an esplanade. It was to be one hundred feet in width at distances from one hundred and fifty to three hundred feet from the existing shoreline, extending from Graves Street to Berkeley. An act had been passed for the collection of dues on all goods loaded and unloaded at Toronto docks to be used to preserve and improve the harbour. This more than paid for the lighthouse keeper's wages; but the balance went into the public purse and was not used on the harbour as intended.

Legal disputes and commercial complaints continued but no adequate legislation was passed to bring the harbour under one central governing body. Many plans were laid, studies made, even contracts awarded, but little was changed until the first railway was built out of Toronto. Then, the city feared that the railways would claim the remaining waterfront properties for their rights of way. Council had to act. Finally, in 1850, an act was passed to provide for future management. Five commissioners were appointed to regulate harbour use, to supervise vessels using the harbour, to levy tolls and to suggest a plan for improvement. A Harbour Master was appointed and he soon presented his first report. The esplanade was built.

When Richard Tinning had arrived from Carlisle, England in 1836, he recognized immediately the importance of Toronto's harbour. He built and maintained a large dock at the foot of York Street and it rapidly became a centre for Toronto's shipping interests. Most of the boats at that time were sailing schooners carrying one hundred tons of cargo, fifty tons below deck and fifty tons above. Grain, oil, sand and gravel, machinery and merchandise from Europe and North America were shipped from and received at Tinning's Wharf. His wharf and enormous warehouses were vital to the industry until 1886 when they were purchased by the CPR and the wharf was demolished. Tinning also maintained Toronto's first lifeboat at his wharf. He and his entire crew provided this service to the city on a voluntary basis.

In February 1853 the first complete breach in the peninsula across the eastern end of the bay occurred during a storm, creating a natural, fifty yard eastern-gap entrance to the harbour. The following year a contract was awarded for excavation of the channel at Queen's Wharf. The commissioners purchased a steam dredge to speed up the process.

Then in the fall of 1858 a disaster hit the small settlement. For some years the deserted governor's house on the sandbar, now known as Toronto Island, had been used by Mr. Privat as a gaming club. Since access was via a barge pulled by four horses on a treadmill, no policemen could raid the establishment without being seen in advance, thus giving the gamblers ample time to clear away any evidence of their activities. One night a violent storm battered the peninsula, separating the sandbar from the mainland and creating Toronto Island. The hotel was swept into the bay.

The city decided to widen the gap caused by the storm, edging it with piles and cribbing. However, because it was only dredged to the depth of twelve feet, the drifting sand continued to create problems for incoming ships. With the increased tonnage of the ships, the building of the Welland Canal in 1881 and its enlargement in 1885, there was a need for a more constantly maintained deeper harbour. It was not until 1902, however, that this was remedied and the depth of the harbour was dredged sufficiently to be maintained at a constant depth. A breakwater was built along the southerly shore of the sandbar to prevent further damage from storms.

In 1895 the movement of the sand from east to west along the shore of the island and north around Gibraltar Point threatened to close the Western Gap into the bay. Additional piling and regular dredging at Queen's Wharf was necessary to keep the traffic flowing. It was not possible to deepen the Western Gap to twenty-four feet because of a rock shelf. It was discovered, however, that the required depth could be obtained by locating the gap thirteen hundred feet south. So a new, wider and deeper Western Gap was created in 1907.

Toronto's harbour was not only important for her commercial interests. She was the seat of much social and sports activity over the years. Aside from being hard workers, the Tinning boys liked to row. In 1858, a challenge was made by a Chicago rowing four. They put up a purse of two thousand dollars, stating that they could beat anything or anyone on the Great Lakes. The challenge was accepted by the Tinnings. Richard Tinning, Junior, acted as coxswain, his brothers, John and Thomas, plus William Dillon and Michael Tweedy formed the crew. They went to Detroit where the race was held and the Tinning crew won quite easily. A number of Toronto notables accompanied the boys on their jaunt, and a great welcome was given them on their return.

Later in the century, Ned Hanlan brought the world singles sculling championship home to Toronto after winning the championships in both Canada and the USA. On his return, Hanlan stood atop the wheelhouse of the *Chicora* and steamed around the bay. Captains were afraid their boats would capsize as everyone leaned out the side of the boats, eager to see the returning hero. There were bands and bunting and streamers on every boat — a regular carnival atmosphere greeted him. It was Hanlan's family who later ran the Hanlan Hotel on the western tip of Toronto Island; his name is today remembered in Hanlan's Point. A pylon was also erected on the waterfront to commemorate his achievements.

A large number of aquatic clubs were established on the north shore of the Bay starting at Simcoe Street. The first home of the Royal Canadian Yacht Club was established there in 1852. East of them was the home of the famous Argonaut Rowing Club and next to it the Toronto Canoe Club. In sporting circles this represented a veritable goldmine in equipment and talent. In the field of sailing, the Royal Canadian Yacht Club had entries in every top sailing event in North America. The Argonaut Club always had entries in the world-class rowing contests. Hanlan Wright had brought home the championship in 1880. In other years, Wright, Pierce and other top contestants competed in singles, tandems, fours and eights.

Our family, like many other Toronto families, grew up with the waterfront. We spent hours watching the boats ply the lake, participating in her sporting and business activities over the years and noting all the changes. In 1900 my two oldest brothers, Alex and Lou, were in the rowing race that was part of the Annual Dominion Day Aquatic Regatta. The bay was full of all sorts and sizes of

Excursion steamer *Chippewa* (Niagara Navigation Company) — 1893-1936

boats with banners and flags flying. A war canoe race between the Balmy Beach and Toronto Canoe clubs was one of the most exciting events of the day. Twelve men pulling in unison made apparent leaps along the water. Those were days long to be remembered.

In the winter, ice rinks between the wharves were kept free of snow for the "roarin' game" as curling was then known. The bay was used for skating and iceboat sailing; cutter racing on the ice was a popular participant and spectator sport.

Initially it was sailing ships that were the most common form of transportation out of the harbour and, even after the first steamship, the *Frontenac*, was launched on Lake Ontario in 1816, sailing ships were used to carry much of the freight. Being steam-powered and much heavier, the steam vessels could contest the freeze-up a little longer and this became an important economic factor.

As soon as there was any sign of spring, the harbour master, whose house was just behind the Queen's Wharf on the Western Gap, would announce the race for his silk hat. The first steam vessel to dock in the harbour would win the silk hat and be saluted by everything that had steam up.

Toronto Harbour had as fine a fleet of passenger steamers as any that plied the Great Lakes. The *Chicora*, put into service in 1879, was the classiest ship on Lake Ontario in its time. It was called an upper-cabin steamer; it was capable of carrying a load of fifteen hundred passengers. It had beautiful interior furnishings in its cabins, more like the later *Chippewa*. She was known for the fine journey she gave her passengers. The *Corona* was an older ship, not quite so luxurious, but she had a busier life in the early days of lake navigation.

The Niagara Navigation Company of Toronto, owners of both the *Chicora* and the *Corona*, also owned a steamer named after the British man-of-war of the Great Lakes in 1812, the *Chippewa*. It was a paddle-wheeler with a visible walking beam, which gave it a very smooth ride. It had two stacks and three decks and a capacity for carrying two thousand passengers. It was built in Hamilton in 1893. The *Chippewa* was the flagship of the fleet and at top speed could run at eighteen knots. In 1906 the *Cayuga*, a faster, bigger boat but not quite as refined, took over from her.

All four of these boats were primarily passenger ships doing a mammoth business. They also had large cargo space.

When I was young, Niagara peaches and other delicate produce was loaded onto these boats after being picked early in the day. They would steam into the Toronto harbour at the end of the day, having crossed the lake carrying a full load. The special cargo was warehoused overnight and sold to customers the next day. Since a damaged basket could not be turned in to the wholesaler, our family was often among those who purchased these baskets for just twenty-five cents.

The *Garden City* and the *Dalhousie City*, two other ships belonging to the Lake Side Navigation Company, were doing the same job from St. Catharines to Toronto with packed loads during the fruit season.

The Hamilton run, with three fine ships, was used more for pleasure or business communications. The *Macassa* did a steady business along this route until the motor car and train wiped out most of its trade.

The Kingston and Toronto passenger ships had

baths for overnight sailing passengers and fine food. This made the trip very pleasant whether you were heading east on business or pleasure. Speed was not the most important thing in our lives then.

Saturday trips across the lake were a common excursion for all of us. They were a grand experience! You could buy a book of tickets and make the round trip for sixty cents a head.

My brother Cecil and I were fond of the lake steamers. One of our joys in these trips was to stare over the bow out of the cabin windows as the east wind churned up the water. On one return trip from Hamilton, the lake was particularly heavy and the first fifteen feet of the bow area was the only part of the deck that was dry. As each wave hit, it would ship some water over the side rails. We timed our movements so that we could be out the cabin door and onto the dry spot on the bow before the wave hit. The Captain soon saw us and, using his megaphone, he called to us from the bridge and ordered us to get back inside the cabin.

When the first railway was built out of Toronto in the 1850s, many of the lake vessels lost business to them. Some, however, gained business, as a large lumber industry was opened up around Georgian Bay for which Toronto and her shipping vessels became the distribution centre. The railways opened up the hinterlands; they also facilitated travel for people and goods in the wintertime.

To avoid the inland route between Hamilton and Toronto which would have required many bridges, the Toronto, Hamilton and Buffalo Line laid a solid foundation on the marshland between Grenadier Point in High Park and Lake Ontario, a track still used today. A landfill was made with rights-of-way for a lakeshore road and a switch for the Swansea Bolt Works. The rail line was built up to the level of approximately ten feet. This build-up was necessary to prevent the erosion of the line which could be caused by the constant battering of southwest winds and rough weather. Each time the land was enclosed in this way, a marsh was formed inland which had to be allowed to flow into the lake.

For some years this line functioned as the Toronto, Hamilton and Buffalo Company and served all the towns and areas in between these three centres. This line was taken over by the Grand Trunk Railway and later by the Canadian government as part of the Canadian National Railways in 1918.

The last half of the nineteenth century was a time of great railway building. Companies were formed, rights-of-way negotiated and rails laid. Profits were to be made in this venture! But in time, economic depression, fierce competition and even the motor car forced many of these companies into bankruptcy. Others were taken over by larger firms or simply allowed to lie unused.

The Belt Line Radial was one such operation. During the real estate boom of the 1880s, a group of Toronto businessmen formed a company which was beset with difficulties from the start. It took them some years to obtain the necessary rights-of-way. When they did, however, they built twenty miles of steam line which followed the course of the ravines up the valley of the Don, crossing Yonge Street north of the Mount Pleasant Cemetery and returning south via the Humber River Valley. A section along the waterfront connected the east and west loops. Like most radial lines, it used a light engine and small car or cars; its main objective was to realize a profit. For some months it was a fashionable diversion. Real estate agents took prospective customers on the line to show them the effects of land speculation and development. The charge was five cents per station or twenty-five cents per round trip. After several months, the venture died and the group went into bankruptcy. The Grand Trunk Railway took over some of their track and many of the rails were torn up to make ammunition during World War One.

As a child, I walked up the Humber River section of the tracks and often wondered where it went. Weeds were growing over everything. I remember the track and rails running up the valley from Swansea on what is now Kingsway South. They crossed Bloor Street and made the grade up the hill to level ground toward Baby Point. There they disappeared. I never remember any traffic on it. A small part of the original tracks through the northeast corner of Forest Hill remains to this day.

Long ago man found out that it was wise to interrupt the race to survive long enough to regain and maintain health and composure. Today, we call this a vacation. Over ninety years ago, a few successful owners of their own businesses in Toronto were talking about getting together and buying some wooded land along the lakefront to use for this purpose. People were beginning to take Saturday afternoons off from their regular businesses. Toronto was hot and muggy in the city summer, and its wealthier inhabitants had for a long time left their main residence in the city to summer elsewhere in a cooler atmosphere.

A pine forest was located twelve miles west of Toronto, just two miles west of Port Credit. It was beautifully situated and it was here at Lorne Park that the businessmen chose to build their summer homes. Some of the original members of this Lorne Park group were the Briggs, Hewitts, Kelks, Lailys, Warwicks, Hendersons, Jephscotts, Ropers, Bousteads, Clarkes, Aikenheads and Watsons. My Grandfather Richey was also one of the committee and he built himself a cottage named Pioneer Villa.

To arrive at Lorne Park you took the Lakeshore Radial to Port Credit or the Grand Trunk Railway Line which stopped morning and evening one-quarter mile out of the park. From either stop, most of us hired the fine old passenger coach run by Tom Leach of Port Credit for the remainder of the journey. He ran regularly to and from the station or wherever you desired to go, rain or shine.

A thirty-room hotel was built at Lorne Park. A water system was put in with a pump house built far enough inland to avoid the rough treatment of the waves on the west end of the park property. The water was then distributed by surface pipe to all the cottages. To protect the hotel from fire, a good-sized water tank was placed on her roof. The caretaker was responsible for making sure that the water tank was kept above three-quarters full as shown on the water-level gauge.

The back sixty acres of the park were set up with two pavilions for rental to Sunday school picnickers and others. My mother's brother, Harry, ran the hotel and sold the picnic permits.

In those days, Sunday school picnics were big events. Shortly after Easter, the day would be set and tickets would be sold. Lorne Park became the most popular spot. Picnic customers had to transport food and possessions to the Brock Street dock at the foot of Spadina Avenue. It was fourteen miles by boat each way from Brock's Wharf to the dock built at

Lorne Park Wharf — 1898

Lorne Park. It was a durable wooden dock built south for over one hundred feet and with a sixty-foot extension at a forty-five degree angle to the west, providing boats docked there with protection against east and south winds. Fine sixty-foot steam yachts would run in there from the National Yacht Club; picnic boats were the other frequent visitors. One of the steamers which carried about three hundred people to Lorne Park picnics was the *White Star*, a sturdy little ship. Many other small steamers were used in this service and, depending on the crowd, the trip both ways would cost forty cents.

It was from this dock that I learned to swim, dive and fish. My brother Alex was a champion swimmer and taught all of us the right form. I can remember clearly the challenge of stepping into the ice-cold water of Lake Ontario.

Swimming for Mother and the other ladies of the family was quite a different matter. The yards of cloth that were part of women's bathing costumes allowed them merely to go through the motions of swimming. They used one of my uncle's empty boathouses to change from street clothes into their elaborate costumes. It was quite a fashion parade as they emerged clad from top to toe in bathing bloomers, stockings, shoes, skirts and shirts of a dark blue material with a white bow tie which held the blouse tight to the neck and reduced the exposure of their bosoms or any other part of their body. The ladies would wade cautiously into the water with plenty of squeals and laughter. When they got out far enough, they would form a circle and bob up and down in the water, making sure their shoulders got wet.

I remember one particular girl cousin who was a trained nurse and very lively. She would strike out periodically to take a spin around without the other ladies. Despite strong efforts, however, she made little progress before she was exhausted.

So, it was with more noise and splashing than swimming, as we boys knew it, that they returned to the boathouse. The number of girls drowned in boating accidents made the dangers of this practice obvious. Women had to be allowed to learn to swim without all of the clothes which hindered them.

The committee used discretion in choosing to whom they would sell lots at Lorne Park. Since Grandfather Richey had been among the founders of the park, he got permission for us to erect a tent on some vacant land on the west side of the acreage, near a swamp that was not too suitable for cottage building. We built a platform there and erected a two-post and ridge-pole tent, fourteen feet by twenty-eight feet, which became our summer home. Mother kept us clean and orderly which helped ensure our acceptance. It was at Lorne Park that our family had its first opportunity for joint commercial enterprise.

We kept the fires in the two north pavilions stoked so that the picnickers had hot water for coffee and tea and, later, for dishes. Picnickers paid us a fee for the service; sometimes they gave us pies or cakes instead of cash and we all enjoyed the desserts. Uncle Harry had a boathouse with eight rowboats for hire. We would help rent out the boats for him at twenty-five cents an hour. He opened an ice cream parlour just next to the hotel, which added to his take from the events and also provided us with more things to do for money. We carried baskets with peanuts, popcorn and gum for sale to the crowd. This provided our junior practice in merchandising.

The Albertsons had a farm on the east side of the

road running up to the railway station and sold fresh vegetables, corn and fruit. They had a strawberry patch and, when the picking was right, we used to get some pocket money by picking at two cents a box. I was never too successful and soon decided that farming was not my way of life.

It is hard to realize that only one hundred years ago, it was customary to mark the boundaries of one's property with a stump or split rail fence, but in our days at Lorne Park there were plenty of these fences. The timbered land would have to be cleared in order to prepare for cultivation. The trunks of the trees would go to the sawmill to be made into lumber and the branches and stumps were hauled to the boundary of the property. When put in place, they produced a formidable barricade. I remember one occasion in which I encountered this fact head on for the first time when I was a child. We were going through the bush when our progress was halted by the stump fence on the east side of the Keith farm. Through the fence I could see quite a showing of muskmelons. The day was hot and the melons looked good. I went carefully through the fence and scrambled back through another opening. As I was crawling back through the fence, a root broke off and out came a swarm of disturbed bees. I dropped the melon in my hurry to avoid painful damage. Already, the two other boys with me were well ahead out of harm's way. Luckily the bees got me for only one sting, but ever since that day I have stayed away from anything resembling a stump fence. Clearly, they offered a fine place for a bees' nest.

A whole program of entertainment would be planned by the cottagers at Lorne Park and we became a part of these plans. The most active lady in the preparation of the fun was Mrs. Arthur Hewitt. Her husband was president of the Consumers' Gas Company. They ran two dances each week, a senior one on Saturday night and a junior one on Wednesday night. If the weather was good, they were held in the pavilions on the ground; but, if it was raining, they were held in the hotel dining room. We kids used to watch all the fun. The best musicians in Toronto were hired to supply the music and they played the piano, harp, violin and bull fiddle. Mrs. Ramsey, mother of Ruby Ramsey-Rouse who played at all the big Toronto parties, was one of the pianists. Charlie Musgrave, another of Toronto's favourite musicians for dances and expensive private parties, was also a frequent performer. They played the Roger de Coverly, schottische, lancers, waltzes and two-steps. I learned the airs of most of the good Viennese waltzes by heart just standing in the gallery and listening to all of it being played. It was a great musical education. As we grew older and taller, some of the girls without male partners would ask us to participate and in that way we learned some of the dances too.

It was customary for the season's program to include two huge bonfires. At the beginning of the summer we would roast weiners and marshmallows and at the end of August we had a huge corn roast. The butter would sit in huge slabs on the table for all of us to slather generously onto the hot corn. These were exciting, well-planned affairs and the food was doubly delicious because of all the other fun. An annual field day was arranged, with games for everybody. My sisters and brother all got their names on the winners' lists but I never qualified because of a game leg.

Among the original cottagers, the Hewitts were

standouts in the social department. Mrs. Hewitt always helped organize the dances and parties and Mr. Hewitt took over the Sunday evening service and singsong in the hotel dining room with excellent results. The Hewitts had two sons. One afternoon, the boys went out for a sail. The wind died down and they were becalmed. They tried to raise help from the shore with no result so the older boy decided to swim ashore. He was a strong swimmer but the water was cold and he never made it. This was a terrible incident in the history of Lorne Park.

One time my brother Cecil and I had quite an adventure out on the waterfront with a canoe. We wanted to deliver our canoe to Long Branch which was about six miles east of Lorne Park toward Toronto. Our brother Lou was visiting there for the weekend with a girl, Ruby Robinson, on whom he had his eye. He thought the canoe would be useful.

The water was slightly rough when we set out, sitting in the bottom of the canoe using two double paddles. We had life preservers aboard in case of trouble. Mother had approved our plans since we had done it lots of times before and we could be expected to be careful. This particular day, however, as we neared Long Branch, a launch came out from the shore to greet us and to rescue us! We thanked them for their kindness, assured them that all was well and delivered the canoe to our brother Lou. We were quite safe, having taken all necessary precautions.

A man by the name of Walter O'Hara was the caretaker for the Lorne Park property. He acted as constable, lamplighter, pumping station operator and patroller of the park at nights and during picnic days. He occupied the cottage just inside the gates. At no time during our short stay did I ever hear of his services being required as a constable.

We used to build a short ladder to get to the lower limbs of the pine tree next to our tent. It was then no effort to climb to the top, and with our Grandfather Duff's naval telescope we could see the time on the old City Hall clock. From our vantage point we watched the lake steamers and the sailing ships, the scows collecting shale for road building and all the other aspects of harbourfront life.

The *Madeline* had been one of the finest schooners of its day. Built in Bronte in 1892, it was used to transport a great deal of equipment for the growing city. Unfortunately she was a sailing vessel and when steam took over, the *Madeline* was demoted to become one of these stone hookers. The hooker would be anchored where there were shale beds, often at the mouth of the Credit River. Men would hook the shale with the rake, and heave it from the punt onto the schooner behind it. This shale was used for road building in the city.

I can still recall the beautiful sixty-foot pine trees at Lorne Park, the early morning salutes of the crows answered by a flock across the marsh on Keith's Farm, a half mile along the shore, the whip-poor-wills in the evening and cicadas in the heat of the noon-day sun. These memories have lived with me over all these years.

When it came time for our departure from Lorne Park, the wonderful days of my junior education were at an end. My two elder brothers could no longer come away with us for the summer. Alex had entered the University of Toronto to take a chemical engineering course and, during his summers off school, he worked for the Ontario government fire-ranging around North Bay. Lou got a job at the Dominion Bank in a small branch at Tilbury, in southwest Ontario. Rosamond had a job in the

Russell Motor Car Company of Weston. So our live-in family got smaller and the luxury of lazy days in Lorne Park summers was gone forever. Returning to the city for school in the autumn was always a sad time for me.

I had been enrolled in Huron Street School soon after my father's death and then, with our move, I started to go to Gladstone Avenue School. I was never a good pupil. Life was the form of schooling from which I learned the most.

The principal of Gladstone Avenue School then was the renowned Alexander Muir, author of the song "The Maple Leaf Forever", and because of my many pranks I encountered him quite often. He was a strong, fair principal, loved by everybody; and the school had a good standing thanks to his efforts.

Drawing cartoons was one of my favourite pastimes and it was one which got me into a lot of trouble. On one occasion, a teacher named Mr. Shantz was the referee when we were playing basketball against our arch rivals, Givins Street School. The game was close and we were down only two points, but Mr. Shantz seemed determined to let the others win. It seemed that every time we got the ball on the move, the whistle would be blown and a foul would be called on Gladstone. The game ended with them two goals ahead, and our gang talking later in the yard thought we had been gypped. I drew a fairly good likeness of Mr. Shantz in his black Christie hat and his black sideburns with a whistle in his mouth calling "Foul on Gladstone". It found its way to the bulletin board and I wasn't very popular.

Later, when I reached Mr. Shantz's room, I was trying to be a good student. It was music class and he told us to pull our music books out and turn to page twenty-seven. Mr. Shantz was no singer but he was trying to lead us. He bumped the tuning fork on the desk and put it up on its edge to give the right pitch. Three times he did this and nobody responded nor sung a note. He blew a fuse and said we were a bunch of clams. This amused me and I quickly drew a picture of the classroom. At each desk, I drew a circle for the clam and up by the teacher's table beside the music stand I drew a big red lobster with a baton in one claw. The boy beside me began to snicker and that drew Mr. Shantz's attention. He came down to my desk and saw what I had done. He grabbed me by the ear and took me down to the principal's office to get the strap.

Mr. Muir heard the case, saw the evidence and drew out the strapbook. He then told Mr. Shantz to go back to take care of the class while he took care of me. I was shaking as he looked at me sternly. Then, he put the strap back in the book, closed it and lectured me, telling me to be respectful to my elders, particularly to teachers. He told me never to do this again and then he opened another drawer, took out a box and gave me a chocolate. A wide smile showed on his face. He had thought it was funny! I heaved a sigh of relief and promised never to do it again. That was the kind of principal that Mr. Muir was; he made you come away from him a better person.

It was another teacher at Gladstone, Miss Burger, who opened my eyes the most. She told my mother that I was the laziest boy in the class and that if I would only work, I might be one of the best. From that time on, I saw what I looked at and listened and heard. I started to think and consider. The rest of the world would be my schoolroom and university. I spent another year and a half in high school and then went off to work.

With our smaller family, we moved from Lorne Park to Mimico Beach for the summers. People lived there permanently, but we only went there to holiday, often commuting to the city for work. At Lorne Park each summer we had to take down and put up our tent and we soon became experts at the job. When we moved to Mimico Beach, we tore up the platform from Lorne Park and took that with us too. We had a lovely lake site where a farmhouse had burned down, just back from the lakeshore road. It was a hundred-foot lot. We should have bought the land because it was selling for seven dollars a foot at the time, but we simply didn't have seven hundred dollars to spare.

We were next door to a gentleman named William Inglis who owned Inglis Refrigerators. He was a little startled to have a tent erected on the lot next to his summer residence, but when he found out our lineage he made us welcome. He had been our grandfather's next door neighbour on King Street many years earlier. He introduced us to the Mimico Beach community. There were many fine families along the beach and my twin sisters, Lillian and Jessie, had plenty of happy associations with the Inglis, the McGee and the Samson girls.

The McGee residence, "Kilcooley", was a grand summer house with spacious grounds, and every Saturday night the gentlemen of the area were invited over to bowl. My brother Cecil and I were invited to join in the activities. Mr. McGee supplied the refreshments of ginger ale, a large tin box of Christie's soda crackers and a big round of cheddar cheese. Mr. McGee was a wonderful host, an extremely friendly man and he gave us a wonderful way to meet this group of businessmen — Mr. R.W. Eaton, Director of the Company, George Wolfe,

Manager of the Grocery Department, Mr. William Bowman, in charge of the Mail Order Department, and several others from Toronto. Mr. McGee worked at Eaton's as Superintendent under Mr. Eaton.

We two boys dressed in clean white slacks and behaved well so we were readily accepted. We got to know the men personally, something which proved valuable in our later business life in Toronto.

In the morning, my brother and I would time our breakfast to be up to the road to catch the early morning radial into the city. At the same time, Mr. McGee's Packard driven by a chauffeur would often turn out of his drive. If they passed us before the radial arrived, they would move to the curb, make a stop and pick us up, taking us right into the city.

In fine weather we would occasionally row our Dean racing shell from the waterfront area across Humber Bay. Mr. Walter Dean was a top-grade craftsman and he owned a small boat-building operation on the southern side of the Lakeshore Road. The Toronto end of the Lakeshore Radial was out in front of the Dean building. Dean's boats were famous, especially his Sunnyside Cruiser, and his racing shell was used by all good paddlers of the time. We were proud of our fine craft and, using two double paddles, we would often arrive at our destination faster than if we had taken the radial.

In 1905 an enthusiastic group of Parkdale men had decided to form a canoe club and my brother and I had become members. They had approached the city and procured six hundred feet of shoreline on lease. The sea-wall project was already on the drawing boards and the club members asked the city to give them the exact location so that they could erect their building. It was built on piles and was valued at $130,000 when it was destroyed by fire.

Cecil and I would dock our Dean racing shell at the Parkdale Canoe Club on our way into the city.

The waterfront was changing rapidly. With the heavier use of the Toronto Bay by industry of all categories, the water was put out of use for pleasure boats. The aquatic clubs had to find a more peaceful location. The Yacht Club moved to the Island, the Argonauts moved to Sunnyside and the Toronto Canoe Club moved east in the bay.

By this time there was a gravel highway along which horse and buggies and the early automobiles and trucks could be driven. Between the railway and the gravel road was the radial car on an eighteen-inch roadway with a two-foot sidewalk. This was called Highway Number Two and ran from Niagara Falls to Hamilton and Toronto. Two parallel concrete sea walls one hundred and fifty and three hundred feet away from the shoreline were soon constructed. A heavy hydraulic dredge pumped the sand and gravel from the lake bottom onto barges and emptied the sand behind the first sea wall to make land. The second sea wall was created to break the lake storms and create a safe navigable harbour for small boats.

Two more stores were built by Mr. Dean's Boatbuilding Company. Mr. Devon rented small rowboats and canoes to the growing numbers of holidayers and Mrs. Maw did a good business, just west of him, selling ice cream and other confectionery.

There was a level-crossing gateman and guard where the road ran up the grade to the junction of Queen and King streets to Ocean House, an early roadside hotel. I knew the gatekeeper at the level crossing well and used to enjoy being with him as the trains ran through there. The Canadian National Exhibition had been built there in 1890; my father had been a ticket seller at the Dufferin gates until his death.

The harbour was becoming increasingly busy. She was being transformed as roads were built into the rapidly expanding city. The increasing use of automobiles made the need for highways greater. It was the Toronto Harbour Commission and the legislation which formed this commission in 1911 which paved the way for the essential changes to come.

Duck's Hotel and Pleasure Grounds at Humber Mouth — 1878

St. Stephen's Anglican Church — Belleview and College Streets — 1858

Drinking fountain and trough — Spadina Avenue and Clarence Square — 1887

Old Trinity College — Queen Street West — 1852

Oil delivery — Wellington Street West — 1900

Toronto Street Railway snowplough — Queen Street West — 1900

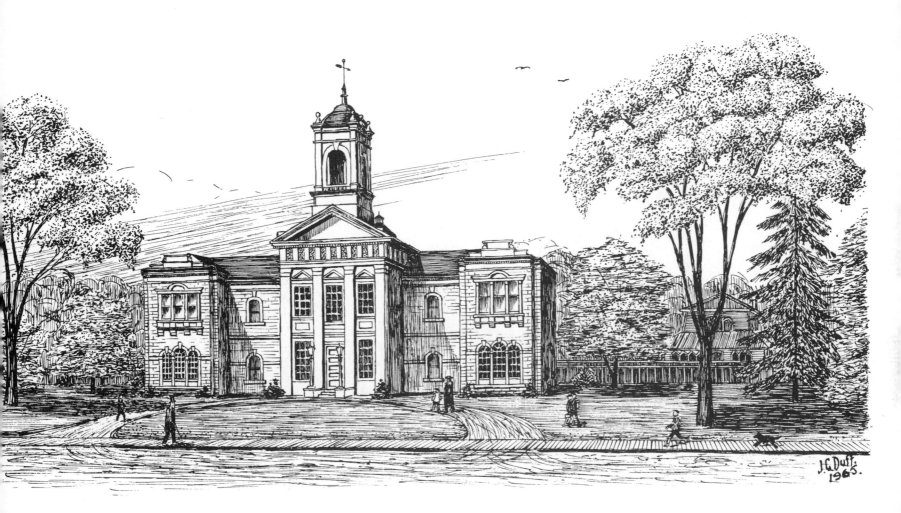

Normal School — Church and Gould Streets — 1852

Metropolitan Wesleyan Methodist Church — Queen and Church Streets — 1872

CHAPTER THREE

The Family Years

Music has always been more important than theatre and other cultural concerns in Toronto, perhaps because of the city's "wholesomeness". This was a quality much admired and sought after in Toronto's early days as well as in my own.

The theatre was under frequent attack for immorality and had little chance to gain a permanent foothold, but music, with its strong religious connections, was part of our daily living. Most of the leading professionals were church organists and choir masters. Pianos were built here because music was such an important aspect of local community life, and the piano provided cheap entertainment. There were good amateur choirs everywhere and singsongs were a part of family life in rich and poor families alike.

One year after I was born, 1894, the Toronto Mendelssohn Choir was formed by Dr. Augustus Stephen Vogt. At first, he started by enlarging his own church group to seventy-five people, and then when he wanted a disciplined singing society "whose tonal quality and expression would resemble that of a fine orchestra" he formed the first Mendelssohn choir. They gave their first concert at the new Massey Music Hall in January 1895, soon after the hall's opening. The concert was a gala affair attended by over eight hundred people. Since that time and with a brief three-year respite while Dr. Vogt reconstituted the choir, it has been performing continuously in Toronto and elsewhere in North America and even in Europe. Each year it is disbanded, and members must audition again in order to be a part of the choir. Yearly, they brought a symphony orchestra to the city before our own was formed by Frank Welsman in 1907 and later, after its disbandment in World War One, in the 1920s. The Toronto Mendelssohn Choir is the oldest performing group in Canada.

Mother had made music an important part of our lives too. No doubt she met our father in her quest for better music. I never heard him sing, but I remember that our musical library had a great deal of choral and operatic music in it. Our piano had a most unusual capacity, something not needed just for a family singsong. It had what you call a transposing shift keyboard.

When the organist at our church decided to make a change, Mother was offered the job. Unfortunately, although she was such a fine pianist, she had no pipe-organ experience. So, it was arranged that she take lessons from Dr. Torrington, "the father of good music in Toronto". He was the organist at the Wesleyan Methodist Church at Queen and Church streets, which was then the leading centre of musical activity in Canada.

After some lessons with him, Mother was given the job at Wesley Methodist Church at a salary of one dollar per Sunday. Boys were also paid something to pump the organ's bellows.

Sundays — church-going days in our household as in so many Toronto households — were sacred. We weren't allowed even to read the newspaper on that day. Our Grandpa Richey was a staunch churchman, a member of the Wesley Methodist Church where we all attended every Sunday morning. In the afternoons, Grandpa would walk from his home to the Don Jail at Broadview and Gerrard to hold an afternoon service for the men in prison. It was a very successful mission.

It was the tradition on Easter Sunday to wear something new or else, tradition had it, you had to watch out for the robins! As fourth boy in the family, I seldom had new clothes. Mostly, I wore hand-me-downs from the other boys. On one particular Easter Sunday though, things were a little different. Because of a sleighing accident earlier in the week, I was wearing a new eye patch! Mother was wearing a new and very fashionable hairdo of which we were very proud. We set out to church as usual that morning with Mother in the lead. Then, Mother caught her heel on a patch of ice just off the front steps and down she went! The bun on top of her head and the backcomb saved the day, leaving her with an imprint on her flesh but, luckily, no other damage. God watched over our family closely and protected us all.

Toronto has been called Toronto the Good through the years. We have a great many lovely churches of all denominations which proves there is something to the name. Because of the large number of British immigrants, the Anglican Church, which received both money and clerical support from England, was influential in our city's early history. Prominent too, though with smaller congregations and less wealth, were the Presbyterian and Methodist churches.

The first Anglican church built here was St. James' Cathedral. Twice it was destroyed by fire before the present building was started in 1850. The architect was fellow Anglican, Frederick William Cumberland, whose own home north of College on St. George Street, formerly called "Pendarvis", is the International Student Centre for the University of Toronto. The spire for the cathedral was built and finished in 1878, three hundred and twenty-four feet high. It commanded the Toronto skyline for nearly a century. My Grandfather Duff, who was a retired midshipman from the British Navy and accustomed to heights, helped put a weathervane on top of the spire. The contractor couldn't hire anybody else to do the task because they were afraid of the height.

Cumberland was the first warden of another early Anglican church, St. Stephen's, on the corner of College and Bellevue. St. Stephen's became known as St. Stephen-in-the-Fields because of its rural setting at the time it was built in 1858. It was built entirely at the expense of Robert Brittain Denison, the third son of Colonel J.T. Denison, an important magistrate in Toronto. The cost was ten thousand dollars. In October 1865 it too burned to the ground, but an enthusiastic congregation rebuilt it and it was reopened only five months later!

The Wesleyan Methodist Church at Queen and Church (now the Metropolitan United Church) was built in 1818. It was the main Methodist Church in the city and contained one of the last carillons in the country. At that time, it also contained one of the largest organs in the world, presented by the Massey family. It was on this organ that Dr. Torrington played. He was a great believer in congregational singing and their Sunday morning service was a perfect way to start the Sabbath day. The home of much of the city's finest music, the church had a fine silver band orchestra and gave tremendous Sunday afternoon concerts.

The Holy Trinity Church, now preserved as part of the Eaton Centre, was built in 1848 from funds donated to the Reverend John Strachan, the first Bishop of Toronto, by two English sisters. It had been made available by the beneficence of Mrs. Margaret Lambert Swale, of Yorkshire, England with the stipulation that it always be called the Holy Trinity Church and that it provide free seats for all. In most of the bigger and more established churches, pews were reserved for those who tithed them. Influence socially, politically and even in education were commonly linked to one's membership in a specific church. Henry Scadding, author of the classic *Toronto of Old*, was Holy Trinity's first rector and a plaque has been erected in his honour on the south wall of the church. His home, a log cabin, once the family home on land ceded by Governor Simcoe in the Don Valley, has been moved to Exhibition Park.

St. John's Garrison Church at the corner of Portland and Stewart streets was built primarily to serve the Stanley Barracks in 1893. So many of the garrison's families attended the church that it became known as the Garrison Church. Also an Anglican church, it was the site of many church military parades. The militia built rows of small houses on several streets from Niagara to Spadina and south of Queen Street to house these families. Although many of the houses still stand today, the church has not survived. In its stead, there is St. John's House, a mission house now serving the area.

So, in 1910 the four corners of King and Simcoe streets represented four aspects of Toronto — damnation at the northeast, which was the home of a tavern; salvation on the southeast, the site of St. Andrew's Church; education on the northwest, the original home of Upper Canada College; and legislation on the southwest, the Lieutenant-Governor of Ontario's home.

It was during this time of church dominance in the city's life that Healey Willan came to Toronto. He became a well-known church organist at St. Mary Magdalene's Anglican Church on Manning Avenue. Before and after his arrival in Toronto, he composed church music, symphonies and other music. He was very influential in early music life here. I've sung many of his anthems here and elsewhere in the world and I've often enjoyed hearing him play. Willan is internationally known for his introits, music which opens a service, and was the only Canadian asked to compose music for Queen Elizabeth's coronation. A plaque has been inscribed for him at the church, St. Mary's, where he made his musical and spiritual home for many years.

Illumination was a very important part of church life as it has always been of home life. The transition from then to now in the provision of reflected light has been remarkable to witness, because growing up in this era included progression from candles to coal oil lamps to electricity. I can still see the row of lamp chimneys that had to be cleaned before I was allowed out to play in the afternoon.

The coal oil merchant made deliveries to most Toronto homes once a week. He had a wagon with a couple of barrels mounted on their sides from which the oil was tapped through a spiggot to our special oil cans. If we didn't have the driver bring it around to our doorsteps with his horse and buggy, we had to go to a store to fetch it. The merchant in the store would fill the can and then stuff a small potato in the spout so we didn't lose any on the way home.

S.S. Kingston — Scott Street Slip —
Toronto Electric Light Plant and Coal Dock
1964

Later came the gas fixtures and the chandeliers and the gas lighting. A fixture would hang from the ceiling in the centre of the room and, on the wall or in a drawer, a long brass rod like a fishing rod with a fifteen-inch long taper fitted into the socket was used to light these fixtures. When this taper was pushed up and lighted, the tap underneath the fixture was turned, releasing the gas. A key was used to turn the gas on and off. It did not produce a very bright flame.

The Bunsen burner which produced a much brighter light was a major breakthrough in gaslight fixtures. It worked similarly to today's kerosene lanterns used for camping and other recreational activities where electricity is not available.

One had to take extra care not to disturb the Bunsen burner in the lamp. The fabric was formed into a cone and, when lit, it was burned off leaving a very brittle mesh which produced a concentrated light. Because it was made of such fine fabric and became so brittle when burned, it was very easily shattered.

Later, came electricity with its beautiful chandeliers and the myriad of new appliances. I remember the excitement we shared with all of the neighbourhood kids. We were the first house on the street to sign up with Toronto Electric Light for domestic electricity. Mother could see that it was a coming thing and she felt it would be much safer for our home. We used to let the kids on the block come in and turn the first carbon lamps on and off, again and again. It was magic!

There were no detergents in those days despite some of the other conveniences and washday was a heavy one. Pure Pears and Sunlight Soap in long square bars had to be cut into cakes with the carving knife and plenty of elbow grease. On sunny days the full clothes lines would blow in the sun and wind. Mother kept up a good front for us with high standards. It meant a lot of hard work for all of us, especially her.

I remember a story which shows the human, very caring side of daily life as it was in Toronto then. It concerns a woman I later came to know as my wife's aunt, Mrs. Will Skeans. One Monday morning, while she was doing her wash, the boiler decided to quit. It had seen years of service but on this particular day, in the middle of the washing operations, it came apart at the bottom so that it could not hold water. The children were all at school and there was no one around to help. So, Mrs. Skeans phoned the hardware and told Mr. May her troubles. She asked if a boiler could be sent over to her. After a bit of silence while he thought about it, Mr. May came up with an idea — to send it out on the next "Toonerville trolley", which ran across her back yard. So, the wash was completed thanks to people's kindness.

Our family operated as a good Scotch clan. Everyone supported each other and there was little quarrelling. Since each of us had separate and quite strong personalities, which were expected to blend into the whole, we had to rely on Mother to sort out our differences of opinion.

Having spent most of our youth in and around the water at Lorne Park and later at Mimico Beach, we were good water rats. In small boats, canoes, rowboats, dinghies and in swimming, my brother Alex gained himself a reputation for his proficiency. He was a strong and active YMCA leader and he undertook to be the best-educated man in our family. He was among the first to enrol in the newly

Canadian Institute — 1890 — later used by the Sons of England — 1910

amalgamated course in Chemical Engineering at the University of Toronto in 1905. While he studied, he used his other skills to support himself financially. First, he served a family in Muskoka as a companion for three growing boys, teaching them swimming, woodcrafts and canoeing. Later, he applied for and got the position as one of the Ontario government's fire rangers and lived in his canoe most of each summer in northern Ontario.

While he was fire ranging through the Cobalt area, he passed a mound of white calcite formation down Rosey Creek. When he returned to town after the summer, he heard rumours of a Cobalt silver find. The rumours stated that the presence of calcite in the formation was advantageous. Al knew where there was a mountain of it! He told somebody about it and word got to Mr. Shaw on Bay Street. In turn, Mr. Shaw contacted Al and things started to buzz.

In return for certain percentages of the find, Mr. Shaw offered to finance a prospecting crew. Al was to take six men and stake out the claims. The deal was good and Al accepted it. He went to his friends in the west end YMCA, picked out the ones he wanted and off they went to Cobalt. There, they found their mound of calcite and staked their claim. Unfortunately, it turned out that Mr. Shaw's money had staked dry land. The silver was under Cobalt Lake! That put an end to our dreams.

I was the only one who profited from the venture. One of the young men that my brother took with him on the expedition was Frank H. Johnston, nicknamed Casey. He was liked by everyone. While the rest of the boys would be staking, Frank would find an elevation with some good scenery, climb out on a rock, get out his colours and his sketch pad and, in no time at all, he would have a fine piece of work to take home with him. He developed into one of Canada's best landscape artists, known as Franz Johnston, for awhile one of the famed Group of Seven.

Many years later, I walked into his studio to show him one of my calendar drawings. He told me it was pretty good, but his parting shot was some advice. He suggested that I take a kitchen chair, draw it, move it, draw it again, move it, draw it again and again. "Do this four times and if it is the same chair, you have succeeded," he told me. By following his advice I was able to improve my perspective.

Meanwhile I was still in school and I had a nasty accident which made me lose a year. I was playing tag in a pair of houses that were under construction. The stairwell to the basement was open with a pile of sand under the opening. I jumped into it and my foot hit a brick which didn't show. This threw my leg and knee out and I was in trouble that has continued since then. A bad case of water on the knee developed. Dr. Todd, our family doctor, was called, but in those days a cure for water on the knee was unknown. A lot of experimenting was done on my behalf. First of all, my knee was packed in hot salt bags to bake the water out through perspiration. Then, hollow needles were used to pump the water out. Antiphlogistine, a paste which induced heat, and fly blisters both worked on the principle of making the knee blister. A small copper mesh chain soaked in iodine was wrapped around my knee and then an electric charge was administered to drive the iodine into the knee. Nothing was accomplished by any of these treatments. Finally, Dr. Todd put my leg in a cast for eleven months, and that almost destroyed my leg. It was during my convalescence that I developed my interest and abilities in pen-and-ink sketching.

Eventually I got out of grade school and entered a technical high school at College Street and University Avenue. Here, they had a science course which included drafting. I applied myself to this closely because I had a distant mission to become an architect.

Our classrooms were on the east side of the old Toronto Athletic Club looking down on the Conservatory of Music. When you opened the classroom window, you were greeted by the sound of song — a lovely lady's soprano voice going diligently over the scales, up and down, up and down until there was a change of key, or the beautiful playing of some concert pianist rehearsing for a performance. It was here that I learned my pitch — listening to the song and its singer rather than the lesson and its teacher! Why study, when you can daydream to such marvellous music? But it was time for me to go to work; we needed more cash flow.

A couple of ambitious men, Don Lindon (who was the Canadian Champion Walker) and Bill Wilson, had been working for Goads Ltd., a firm which produced maps of all the cities and towns of Canada for the insurance companies. The buildings were all blocked in and tinted to show their construction materials. Goads Ltd. was doing a big business with no competition.

My two friends Don and Bill felt they could horn in on this market. They hired some young draftsmen to assist. I was one of these and I left school to take the job. After six months had passed, however, their money ran out and I was out of a job.

It seemed to me that the most likely place to be using an architect at that time was the T. Eaton Company because they were expanding. I went to see my friend from Mimico Beach, Mr. Harry McGee, to see what he could suggest. He was the superintendent in charge of all contracts and he worked closely with Mr. Gouinlock, the Eaton's official store architect. Mr. McGee greeted me like a friend and asked me if I were looking for work. It was a month before Christmas and they were hiring a lot of extra help. Nevertheless, I told him "No."

"I came to see if you would persuade Mr. Gouinlock to give me an apprentice job. I think I'd like to be an architect."

Thinking it a swell idea, he reached for his phone, called and told Mr. Gouinlock that he had a young friend who wanted a job as an apprentice to an architect. Fate had obviously decreed another path for me, however.

"Harry, at this time of year we have laid off good qualified draftsmen until the spring when work picks up again. If the lad will contact me again later on, I would be happy to take him on then."

Once again, Mr. McGee asked me if I wanted a job and, when I replied in the affirmative, he suggested that I go over to Albert Street to the employment office there and ask for Mr. Price. He agreed to arrange for me to work in men's furnishings since I thought I knew most about that area of merchandise.

Over at Albert Street, there was a queue of about two hundred people, all looking for jobs. I envisioned a long wait. Across the room was a wicket with a girl behind it and nobody talking to her, so I made my way over there. But she called out, "If you're looking for work, you had better line up with the others."

My contact with Mr. McGee again helped and

soon I had filled out an application for Mr. Price and was to start work on the Monday. It was Thursday afternoon and I was due at Technical Night School Chemistry Class. Just that day, a gentleman from Consumers' Gas Company had asked our teacher if they had a young man who might be sent over to them as a junior assistant chemist. This sounded more interesting to me than selling ties, so I didn't ever start work at Eaton's. I went instead to Consumers' Gas.

The head chemist was a real gentleman, Mr. Wilfred Philpott. He was a good instructor and I caught on to what was required quickly.

My main job, aside from taking readings on meters and gauges all around the plant, was to make a daily examination of the manufactured gas for heat and candle power. When the coal was shipped in, each load had to be checked for grade. With the yard man assisting, we would take a sample from five different cars, crack it up in our test room and fire it in a test retort. Then I would measure and qualify the gas emitted and okay the train load. I enjoyed the work and stayed there for two years.

In 1909, my brother Al had graduated from the university with a degree in Chemical Engineering. He was in love with a girl in Toronto so he joined the staff of Continental Rubber Company of the US, where he received good money for his work. First, they sent him off to Torreón, Mexico to work in their *guyle*, the rubber plant. After a time there, they decided to explore the headwaters of the Amazon River and Al accepted the challenge of leading the expedition from Quito, Ecuador, heading over the Andes Mountains to the mouth of the Amazon. As far as can be determined, he was the first white man ever to make the trip. He had countless hair-raising adventures, met with tribes of head-hunting Indians and saw many stacks of skulls. It was exciting but it had taken him far away from Toronto, and by the time he returned his sweetheart had married someone else. He was tremendously upset and withdrew into his shell.

When he returned, he obtained a job in the Dunlop Tire and Rubber Company in their engineering department. We had moved from Lisgar Street to Fern Avenue, as usual maintaining our family thrift. By then, three of the eldest children were working. We had our new home in the York Loan District.

Al lived with us, west of Roncesvalles Avenue, a long way from his place of work east of the Don River. To avoid the streetcar ride he bought himself an Indian single-cylinder motorcycle for transportation.

He enjoyed the machine very much and joined the Indian Motorcycle Club on Spadina Avenue. The club took rides out through the country every weekend. The twin-cylinder crowd would let the single-cylinder riders get away ahead of them and then overtake them, leaving them behind as if they were sitting still. Al didn't like to be left behind so he would stick with the twin-cylinder riders. He seemed to have very little difficulty doing it.

The club also ran motorcycle races at Exhibition Half-Mile Track three or four times a season. The last meet was to be for the Ontario Championships. Al knew his engine was good. We knew the times of the riders for the track and decided that I should go down to the track some morning to see what time Al could do. With the permission of my boss at the gas company, I borrowed the stop watch that we used in our work and down we went to the track for the trial. We put Al's machine around the track several times feeling the pull of the turns. Finally, he told me to time him. He had no difficulty matching and beating the record times in existence. Al got a heavy old pair of trousers, put them on, learned to skid and signed up for the last track meet.

Meanwhile, Al talked to his co-workers at the Dunlop Rubber Plant and had them make a change in the design of the tire treads. They created an anti-skid tire especially for him. The last race meet of the season found Al a competitor. He entered the full card — the amateur, the two-mile, the five-mile and the ten-mile. The latter was for the Ontario championships.

Al came first in all the races, lapping the field in the five-mile race. I was in the pit with him and I was pretty proud. Before the last event, however, the management came to him.

"For heaven's sake Duff, the crowd didn't come to the track to see a parade. Please make this last event a race."

Al obliged. He lost ground on the turns, over-throttled the engine to make it sound like engine trouble and until the next to last lap in the last race, the spectators were standing on the chairs as happy as could be, unsure of the outcome. Never had they seen such a race! They gave Al a standing ovation when he came in first, making him the Ontario champion. Abruptly, he decided that this was not his life and he never raced again. Cole and Barabeau, who were two professionals on the track, said they would like to take a crack at him but Al continued to enjoy his motorcycle only at his own speed.

With our move to the York Loan District, our family decided to attend the Galley Avenue or North Parkdale Methodist Church and I decided to attend the Howard Park Church where I had some young friends. The Dunlop family had been former members of Wesley Church and they asked me to join them. I started in the Young Men's Bible Class, then joined the church and the choir. In the choir, I met my future wife, Ruby Skeans, a charming young lady, a good piano player with a fine soprano voice. What more could a young man on the lookout expect to find? I did not look any further.

Our friends all worked in the choir and Sunday School. Ruby played the piano and taught in the Primary Department. I ran the projector for the screen and also lead the hymn singing whenever necessary. We had an attendance of about eight hundred children and a five-piece orchestra. It was a rewarding effort for a Sunday afternoon. After the evening service most of our gang would meet at Ruby's home for a rousing singsong, a nice piece of cake and a cup of tea. The Skeans were good hosts, always making us welcome.

Their family had come of good British stock. Ruby's father and mother had been married by Reverend Hinks at the Broadway Tabernacle, then a popular church in the city, located at College Street and Spadina Avenue where it still stands. The Skeans family had run a produce store at King and John streets. When he closed the produce store, John Skeans developed the Banquet Tea Company on Yonge Street. As it grew, he moved to 503 College Street, where he bought the entire block of stores. He was a great believer in brick and mortar.

After a couple of years, I was still working at the Consumers' Gas Company but I seemed to be going nowhere. I had learned fast from visible observation and I suggested to my boss, Mr. Philpott, that I thought it would be good for me to transfer up to the

Commercial Sales Department at head office on Toronto Street. It seemed like a good step up in the company for me.

The superintendent of gas company employees was a Mr. Jeffries. Our office, the technical division, made our reports to Toronto Street and neither Mr. Philpott nor any of us had considered that we were under Mr. Jeffries' authority. His jurisdiction was Station B. At this juncture, he decreed that everyone within the plant walls had to punch a time clock. We had never done this before but, rather than complain to Toronto Street, we complied. Mr. Jeffries had come up in the company through the machine shop. He was apparently a good man because he now drove an elegant red-painted, brass-trimmed 1907 McLaughlin car with his own chauffeur!

Our lab was a brick lean-to attached to one of the retort houses. Mr. Jeffries would walk in and out each morning just to see that we were busy. We would greet him with "good morning" and his reply was only a grunt, as if we were not worth his talking to at all. This went on indefinitely and one day I told the other assistant chemist that if Mr. Jeffries did not want to talk to us, then I would pay attention to my work and stop greeting him. This may not have been a wise decision.

When I had told Mr. Philpott about my desire to join the Commercial Sales Department, he had expressed his disappointment at the prospect of losing me. Nonetheless, he approved of the idea and suggested that he would tell Mr. Jeffries what I would like to do and that he would look after it for me.

Two months later, I enquired of my boss if anything had happened. He replied that Mr. Jeffries must have forgotten; I suggested that I would see about it myself. He warned me to be careful. I knew Mr. Hewitt, the general manager, well so I went up to Toronto Street. Unfortunately, Mr. Hewitt was out of town for a few days and his secretary suggested that I might see Mr. Armstrong, the company secretary. This I promptly did; I told him my plan and he thought it was a sound idea. It was Thursday afternoon. On Friday afternoon my discharge notice was in my pay envelope.

I had never been fired before or since that time. It was a terrible shock to me and my family, and to my sweetheart, Ruby. I had started paying particular attention to her. Apparently, I had passed family inspection earlier in that same week. I had purchased tickets for us to sail across the lake on Saturday afternoon. When I phoned Ruby to tell her my news, I suggested that the trip be delayed. She disagreed.

"It is Saturday and there is nothing you can do until Monday, anyway. Besides, Mother has packed a lovely box lunch for us to eat at suppertime."

Saturday was a lovely day. I called for Ruby and took her and our box lunch to the quay at the Niagara Navigation Dock at the foot of Yonge Street. As soon as we were on board, we went up to the front deck and ran into another old Mimico Beach friend, Ron Starr, plus his wife and sister-in-law. He was an electrical engineer at the Hydro-Electric Construction Office on Duncan Street. After introductions and greetings were over, Ron suggested that we pull over a couple of chairs and explore the past and future. The first thing Ron asked me was where I was working, so I told him the whole story. He was enraged because he knew my character; he knew I had been hurt by the experience.

"He's a mean old so-and-so. . ." he said in different words. When he saw that I was really upset at being fired, he went further.

"Mr. Jeffries may have been afraid of this young and ambitious youth being in the way of his progress in the gas company so he put the skids under your progress."

His comments made me feel better. We had a lovely trip over to Niagara, ate our excellent box lunch on the hurricane deck and I made progress in my love affairs on the way home. Then Mr. Starr asked if I would like a job as material clerk in the Hydro Construction Department.

Thanks to him I never lost five minutes' work. I started at Hydro the following Monday morning. My knowledge of drafting made it easy for me to read blueprints and plans and I had sufficient knowledge to handle requisitions on the job schedule. I soon caught on and was useful.

My last job at the gas works had been to check the gradual increase of temperature in the bank of new retorts in a retort house at Station B. The process was to increase the retorts' temperature at a slow enough pace not to crack them. We entered the area each morning where a workman opened the retort loading doors and, with a pyrometer, measured the intensity of the heat. The retorts were stacked in banks three high and we tested them all, recording the degrees of heat in each. It was very precise work.

Two weeks after I left the job, the young lad whom I had had as an assistant was continuing the recording. Then, one morning the workman opened the doors and there was a terrible explosion. Three men were killed, including the lad who was doing my old job! This gave me some deep thoughts. I wondered if God had purposefully cleared me out of the way and that it was not my time. I still had work to do on Earth. Our family had been brought up as good Christians believing in God's power to protect us and keep up safe. There have been other incidents in my life to substantiate this belief.

For two years I worked for Hydro going to night school to study business management and book-keeping. In this time I gained favour with Ruby and my father-in-law to-be and he asked me to join his business. He ran a successful business called the Banquet Tea Company which primarily sold tea, but also coffee, spices and jelly powder. He had seven salesmen with horses and wagons and they covered forty-two routes city wide on a six-day week, starting at seven-thirty each morning.

Our men got twenty-five dollars per week with a commission on the sales over a certain amount. My job was to canvas for new business, getting as much business as possible from the territory without increasing the overhead. I was also spare man on the routes, chief canvasser and tea blender. We had all to take it in turns in working on the seventh day, because the horses needed to be fed and watered daily whether it was Christmas Day or Sunday.

Our shop was three storeys plus basement, and the horses and wagons and sleighs were kept in the rear at 503 College Street. The basement was full of the chests of tea. An elevator moved the chests up to the third floor to the blending mill and then down a shoot to the packaging area on the main floor.

We gave a sales coupon with every ten cents of purchase and a coupon book into which to paste the stamps. We ran a premium store and gave a good premium on the whole book if the customer owed nothing on her account. This worked splendidly and ours was practically a cash business.

Our main opposition was the Ocean Blend Tea Company and they had about twenty-five vehicles. Their sales method was to convince a householder to take in a small caddy of tea. A few days later they would return and try to collect the money for it. This put a tremendous amount of credit on the books and their overhead was high.

I usually started at 9 a.m. after dishes had been done, and when the householder had had a chance to get herself a bit organized. I would look through the glass and if I saw movement in the kitchen, I knew someone was at home. If I found no one, I would return another day.

On one particular day I looked, saw someone but had no reply to my continued knocking. Finally, the lady in question dropped her apron. "I'm canvassing for the Banquet Tea Company," I began politely.

"And I'm canvassing for the washtub," she replied and slammed the door in my face!

Next door, I managed to sell a pound of coffee and was glad that it wasn't going to turn out to be a total loss of a day. As I left the house, the lady from the other house came down the sidewalk. She was apologetic and, before I had left, she ordered a pound of tea. In those days, we sold coffee for eighteen cents a pound and tea for three pounds for a dollar.

I was a professional doorbell ringer and I didn't come across many rebuffs. I was polite and grammatically correct in my speech. This was always important in the job.

I was never afraid of work and saw that I was destined to be a salesman. My wife-to-be and mother gave me encouragement and there were no other children in the Skeans family so I had the field to myself if I fitted in successfully. This I did. Business

was good and I could handle it. For Mr. Skeans, this was the test.

Meanwhile the rest of Toronto was also prospering and growing. Henry M. Pellatt had been born in Toronto and attended the Model School on Church Street in the same class as my father. His greatest asset was his determination, something he learned while he was still at school. Smart at his books, he was also extra smart at athletics and always wanted to be the first in each event. He held over fifty medals and prizes in school and at the age of nineteen he had gone down to the Athletic Club in New York to challenge the American owner of the mile record, Mr. McDuffy. Despite the fact that the Americans had entered three men in the race, thinking that the two extra men would make it more difficult, Pellatt set too fast a pace and soon these two dropped out of the race. Pellatt and McDuffy entered the last lap abreast. Again, Pellatt proved too fast and he walked away with the prize. His time was four minutes, thirty-one seconds. It was 1879.

By the early twentieth century, Pellatt was the owner of about thirty business firms and mines; he had the Midas touch and amassed a large sum of money. He was a Britisher and a very faithful Colonel of the Queen's Own Regiment.

Sir Henry was knighted by King Edward on November 8, 1905, for his loyalty as a Canadian and for his financial generosity in taking the Queen's Own Regiment, seven hundred strong, over to London. His visit to Buckingham Palace and the parade of his troops was all at his own expense. Sir Henry's favourite mount was in the parade and he was offered ten thousand dollars for it.

Casa Loma — Austin Terrace — 1914

As well as being a successful businessman, Sir Henry was also a dreamer. It seemed to him that trouble was always brewing in Europe and he worried that it might put the royal family in danger. He decided that they must have a suitable building in Toronto to which they could retreat; as well, the city needed a suitable place to entertain them when they came for a visit.

So, Mr. Pellatt purchased land from the Austins which had originally been a part of the Spadina estate on the escarpment. He gave his building a lot of thought. He hired Toronto's best architect, E.J. Lennox, the man who had designed City Hall, and the two of them made an extended tour of Europe examining the architecture of the finest castles anywhere. Mr. Lennox made hundreds of sketches, both practical and ornamental; Mr. Pellatt busied himself buying marble and equipment for thirty fireplaces. He planned a palace with massive stables for his favourite mount.

After various financial setbacks and an attempt to close off certain public thoroughfares around his properties which failed, Pellatt had construction begin in 1910. The stables were to be built first. There were stalls for ten horses plus a large carriage area, all of it tiled. The heated stables were connected to the main castle by an underground passageway. They were completed before construction of the castle was begun.

Mr. Pellatt loved horses, particularly his favourite mount, and was very disturbed when his veterinarian noticed that this horse was failing. He was not grinding his oats properly and, on examination of the teeth, the veterinarian determined that they were the source of his trouble. So it was decided to manufacture a set of false teeth for him.

The experiment had some success and the horse gained weight for a short time. Eventually, however, he starved to death. This set of teeth was kept in a glass case in the castle for some time, but at some point was stolen.

Sir Henry spared no expense in construction of his castle and stables. The ceiling in the main foyer of the castle is sixty feet above the floor. There was a twenty-six by forty foot billiard room with a full-sized table in it. The parlour is panelled in carved oak. There was an elevator and hall leading to the kitchens and pantries, which are an exact duplicate of those in Windsor Castle. There were over ninety rooms, with fireplaces galore and a full basement with swimming pool, shooting gallery and wine cellar, plus the entrance to the boiler room and stable. The tunnel to the stable was 800 feet long. It was reported that it required five tons of coal a day to heat the place when it was fully occupied.

The main tower on the corner stands one hundred and twenty feet above the grounds. The stone fence around the five-acre site was created by the use of ordinary fieldstone and an artful use of concrete for columns. Sir Henry made it known that he would pay the farmers a good price for each field-stone delivered to the premises and he imported Scottish stonemasons to create the fence at a cost of $250,000. The landscaping of the grounds with ornamental trees and flowering shrubs was beautiful. A uniformed doorman helped people out of their cars at the entrance of the castle.

In 1914, the dreamer, Sir Henry Pellatt, finally took up residence in his dream castle.

Meanwhile, baseball had prospered in the city, first being played at Diamond Park and then being moved

Toronto General Hospital — Gerrard Street east of Parliament Street — 1854-1921

over to the Island. Some of the great names included Dick Rudolph, a home-run hitter of great repute, and Bunny Hearne, who could pitch a mean game. We attended games whenever we could. I was an avid baseball fan but when I started working for the tea company I had to work long hours and couldn't find the time to watch any sports.

In 1911 the Toronto Harbour Commission had been formed with jurisdiction to coordinate the development of the Toronto harbour. It had to be able to accommodate ever larger ships; eventually the seagoing ships would need to dock there.

The harbour was to be dredged to a depth of twenty-four feet. At the west end to replace the Western Gap, a ship channel was excavated with a circulating channel connecting the deep water of the bay with the open waters of the lake. A sea wall and breakwater along the western and eastern lakefronts of the city were built and a moveable bridge, Cherry Street Bridge, was constructed over Keating's Channel, entrance of the Don River into the Bay. Retaining walls were built to confine these waterways and a portion of the retaining wall of Keating's Channel was built. The reclaimed land was to form part of a new industrial area, the Toronto Industrial Area in the former Ashbridge's Bay district, where all of the dredged material was dumped. Federal, provincial and city governments cooperated on the massive project. Permanent lifesaving and police patrol services were established.

Railway tracks would serve all dock areas. The great fire of 1904 had levelled so many buildings that it was possible for the railway company to purchase enough land to build Union Station down on Front Street. It was finally completed in 1919.

Transportation was a vital issue to the growing city since manufacturing had become such an important industry to Toronto. It hastened the improvement of all transportation facilities within the city and routes leading into the city.

Highways had to be improved as private automobiles became more numerous. The Toronto-Hamilton Highway was undertaken with Toronto, Hamilton and the counties in between each paying a portion of the cost. As advertising implied, there were more cars for sale. In 1904 the Hyslop Brothers advertised themselves as the Oldsmobile agents; they also sold Cadillacs, which were lower priced than other imported luxury cars. Russells were built here and my sister, Rosamond, worked for the manufacturer for a time. Henry Ford's operation was expanded and his cars were made cheaper and easier to purchase. In 1902, Toronto street traffic by-laws had been amended to include cars. In 1912, the speed limit according to Dominion Statutes was set at fifteen miles per hour. I can remember my father-in-law being fined for going seventeen miles per hour under the King Street subway.

Between 1904 and 1913 the number of building permits within the city had multiplied greatly. St. Paul's Church on Bloor Street and the General Hospital on University Avenue were built. Individual barons of industry wielded a lot of commercial and other power, but the population had grown and the city had expanded outwards. People living in the outlying districts and working downtown were plagued by poor transportation service. The Toronto Railway Company refused anything but one-way tickets to the city limits as they had been established in 1891. It was costly and confusing. The public clamoured for better service and the city was forced to establish the Toronto Civic Railways in 1911 to

The Armouries — University Avenue — 1891

run its own streetcars in addition to the privately owned and operated system which had previously enjoyed the monopoly.

The tea business, however, still operated with horse-drawn carriages and sleighs in the winter. I remember one day at the end of February when one of our men was sick and I had to take his route. The winter had been pretty severe, with lots of snow. The horses were fitted out with winter shoes which had sharp caulks hammered on to them to keep them from slipping on the ice. There was no snow removal then, although the transit system ran a snow plough along its tracks to keep them clear. The heavy snows of that winter were piled higher along the edges of the tracks than on the rest of the road.

Our sleighs were completely open with the merchandise stored in wooden boxes covered with a tarpaulin. It was snowing hard, I was cold and glad that I had only a few calls to make before heading back to the store on College.

I was going east on Queen Street, passing the long brick wall on the south side of Queen Street West in front of the asylum where the snow was drifted against the wall. My sleigh hit a bump and swerved down onto the car tracks. The left side dropped about a foot and bent the runner on the front of the sleigh. Luckily it did not spill right over but the sleigh and I were tipped precariously like a ship on a stormy wave.

With help from passing people, I got the sleigh off the car tracks in time to let the streetcar pass but I had to repair the runner before I could resume my journey homeward. Luckily too there was a hardware store, conveniently opposite, run by a fellow member of our church and he was able to give me some wire and a piece of scantling with which I could temporarily repair the runner. This type of accident was not that unusual at the time, with the confusion caused by the increasing traffic, the poor roads and the strange assortment of vehicles on the road — horse-drawn sleighs, cars, trucks, streetcars and even bicycles.

I experienced another accident some months after this which involved yet another near collision of two vehicles. It was one Saturday afternoon in the spring and Al had accepted an invitation to motor up to Hamilton with friends. He suggested to me that I might like to use his motorcycle. I thought it would be swell since I had been invited to Ruby's for supper. Because the handlebars were too wide to get through the side gate at our place on Fern Avenue, it was kept at a garage on the east side of Roncesvalles. I put on my good togs and went over to the garage, feeling chipper and on top of it all.

I pulled the Indian cycle out of its stall and set it up on its stand in the rear of the garage. I turned on the ignition and kicked the starter pedal; and the engine started. The clutch stick was forward and I tried in vain to pull it back. It wouldn't slide, so I tapped it with my fist and I was on my way out of the door before I realized it. We ran too close to a parked car and headed into the alley. It was a Russell motor car and its rear fender stuck straight out. I missed the car but caught the motorcycle's cable, which was the gas control, on the extended fender. It pulled apart with the gas on full. We headed straight across the road, hit the curb with enough speed to clear the sidewalk and landed in a nice mud puddle with the engine roaring. Luckily, there had been no traffic on Roncesvalles! Finally, I got the machine stopped and wheeled it back to its berth. Nothing was broken nor even bent, just muddied. I cleaned it

85

up as best I could, returned home to wash up, donned one of Al's second-best suits and headed over to Ruby's home via the streetcar. Al only laughed when I told him the story, proof of his generosity and gentle spirit.

Lou and Cecil, my two older brothers, had gone out to Carlstadt, Saskatchewan to try their luck at homesteading. Our Uncle, John Morrisson, originally from Weston, had already established a successful farm out there around Yellowgrass. The two boys each took a half-section of land and lived together in a shack backing onto the two properties. Neither was successful in farming, however, and they left to join the CPR.

During this happy period of growing up for Toronto and myself, four of us couples had spent all our time together going from one house to another, one picnic to another. We were eight people in love, all of us young. One of the boys, a medical graduate from the University of Toronto, Archibald McCallum, named us the OCTO LAETĒ or the Joyful Eight. Of the eight friends, only Ruby and I married.

Up until 1913 the Toronto Militia Organizations had put on sham battles for the educational benefit of the general public and to introduce them to the military. These glorified military manoeuvres were generally held in the Riverdale Flats on Dundas Street, at the Christie Pits and at High Park, and were traditionally held to celebrate the Queen's birthday on May twenty-fourth. The locations provided hill slopes from which the public could get a good view of the goings-on and there was plenty of excitement. Sides would be chosen, a boom would sound from a fieldpiece and the men would run for cover. There would be a rattle of musketry, a heavy pall of gunpowder smoke and the manoeuvres of battles, each group claiming wins or losses of territory. Finally, somebody would be declared the winner. Bands played, troops marched past and the day was climaxed with a big fireworks display. It was great fun, but in 1914 the world no longer needed sham battles and the practice was stopped.

Things changed radically with the declaration of World War One. Sham battles, our peaceful social life and the prosperity of the city were halted.

Both of my brothers still out west, Lou and Cecil, enlisted immediately. Cecil was attached to the 203d Battalion of Winnipeg and, upon being sent overseas, was transferred to the head office in London because he had suffered from rheumatic fever. He remained there during the entire war. My brother Lou, however, was sent into the field with the 18th Battalion from Moosejaw. During some heavy artillery fire of the newly sandbagged trenches in which he was fighting, a shell caught him on the head and he was carried out for dead. Aside from shattering the bowl of his ever-present pipe and creasing his forehead with shrapnel, the shell severed his right ear. Although it was surgically re-attached, he never recovered his hearing. My brother Alex was kept in Canada with the Munitions Section of the forces where they could utilize his chemical engineering expertise. I was never accepted in the forces because of my game leg.

Our medical friend, Archibald McCallum, joined the Royal Canadian Navy in 1916. He became a surgeon on board several of the destroyers, one of the first doctors ever to do this.

Growth and development were halted in the city. Railway tracks were torn up for steel for ammunition. Thousands of men were shipped off to war. Many never returned.

Queen's Hotel — Front Street at University Avenue — 1862

Frogley's Bakery — Yorkville Avenue and Yonge Street — 1881

Red Lion Hotel — Yonge Street north of Bloor Street — 1808

Chute-the-Chutes — Scarborough Beach Park — 1907-1925

CHAPTER FOUR

The Business Years

The war saw many changes for Toronto as it did for all of the world. Life continued in the city at a slower pace with an acute labour shortage as more and more men and women were taken into the armed forces. Women came into the labour forces in greater numbers. Materials, such as steel and gasoline, were also in short supply and manufacturing was severely limited except for the production of the necessities of war.

It was 1917 that proved most significant for me. In that year, the government introduced income tax as a "temporary measure" to help fund the war effort and to help subsidize the road building to which they were committed. They also introduced conscription and, finally, votes for women. Long accustomed to independent working women, the latter was not a difficult idea for me to accept.

Most important to me, my courtship of Ruby Skeans had progressed and we were married on June 30th of that year by Reverend Hinks, the same preacher who had married Ruby's parents. With this marriage I gained a whole new family. Mr. Skeans loved his wife and only daughter and, the Christmas before we were married, he had given each of them a mink coat. He had also built a pair of houses on Glendonwynne Avenue so that his wife and daughter could remain close after our marriage. However, we never did live in these matching houses. Instead, we all lived in the house on Boustead Avenue from which we were married. It was a large three-storey house and there was plenty of room for all of us.

Ruby's mother was a wonderful lady — happy, intelligent and statuesque, and I loved her as I did her only daughter, Ruby. Mrs. Skeans was an excellent cook who could whip up a plate of hot biscuits and other delicious foods in a matter of minutes, never needing to measure any of the ingredients. She was in charge of the kitchen. Mr. Skeans, my father-in-law, had proven his success in business and I willingly absorbed many of his ideas because I had no living father of my own from whom to learn. He tolerated me because I had enough good qualities to be almost necessary. I was given full charge of the garden and I made sure it was landscaped beautifully. For four to five months out of the year, the Skeans would go to Florida with friends leaving us with the house to ourselves. It was on one of these trips that Mr. Skeans made a discovery that caused us to change our business.

After Ruby and I were married, however, and for my first real two weeks of holiday, we went off to Jackson's Point on Lake Simcoe and Bala in Muskoka, both popular vacation spots with Torontonians who could afford holidays. My father-in-law had cautioned me that neither he nor his daughter could swim nor were particularly confident around water. It was a fact I would have done well to remember.

We had passed a lovely week at Jackson's Point with warm weather, and the day before we were to leave for Bala, my Aunt Elizabeth, who happened to be staying in the same hotel as us, organized a boat ride to Georgina Island as a treat for us. Saturday dawned hot and clear. The party included ten women and two men, plus the owner of the open fishing boat. The motor was a two-cylinder St. Lawrence, a dependable motor. The boat had a bench seat all around its edge where all the passengers sat.

We took off all right, full speed, and headed for Georgina Island, the local Indian Reservation. There was only a makeshift wharf to which to tie the boat and the boatman secured it there as the ladies and the other men started to walk up onto the shore.

I stayed behind with the boatman. I felt the weather closing in and noticed that it was dark on the southwest horizon. When I mentioned this to the boat operator, however, he didn't seem disturbed. Then, I heard the distant sound of thunder. Although I had never been on Lake Simcoe before, I recognized that a storm was brewing.

The boatman called the others back and, with all of us aboard, we set out immediately. Just about two hundred yards out, the squall started to show on the surface of the water. The storm was coming from the southwest. There were four sticks raised up over the engine and only an oil cloth stretched over this to keep the engine dry. There were no life preservers aboard; the women, including my wife, did not know how to swim; and the man had no licence and little skill in running the boat. He asked me if I knew anything about boats and I told him that I had had lots of experience.

"Keep the engine dry and running slowly," I managed to shout to him before the storm broke. I took the wheel in the bow. Rumbling thunder echoed across the lake and sheets of rain poured down on us. I assured the ladies that we would make the shore safely, but they were praying and crying.

I was able to quarter the waves and we made it to shelter under the bridge until the storm was over. Nonetheless, it had been a rough ride and a frightening one for everyone. There were no regulations of any sort on pleasure boating in those days, and the boatman had less experience than myself on the water. Since then, I have always used my own judgement on the weather. We should never have gone. I never did tell my father-in-law about this incident, thankful that it had ended as it did.

Back in the city, many of those who returned from the war returned to a changed environment. Cars and trucks were making their presence felt increasingly in business. In 1898, Robert Simpson had imported an electric-powered truck to supplement his famous matched grey-horse teams which delivered his goods. Although the truck was ahead of its time and did not make any significant impact on business practices, it was a good publicity stunt and an indication of things to come. In 1899, Parker Dye Works bought an electric delivery wagon which had been built in Toronto. When this truck was involved in an accident in July of that year, it may have been the city's first accident involving a truck.

The war had taught many of its personnel, particularly those who had served in the Army Service Corps, about the transportation of goods and bodies first by horses and later by trucks. Men saw the advantages of moving freight with these motor vehicles; they came to love them; they also learned how to keep them running efficiently. So, after the war, many of them returned to their homes in Toronto and surrounding small towns and established various trucking companies, generally by purchasing one vehicle. In those days, Model T Fords could be converted to trucks for the small cost of a three-hundred-and-fifty-dollar conversion kit. In their trucks, the men made pick-ups and deliveries themselves and became independent. They gained respect and business.

Mr. Hendrie, whose family had run a horse-driven cartage business since 1855, was presented with a truck by his wife on his return from the front. His company, Hendrie and Company Ltd. of Toronto, is now the oldest cartage firm in the business. Many other companies were formed at this time; it was the birth of the trucking industry.

Roads were poor, however, both inside and outside the city. Records from the City Council meetings in 1913 record various discussions about "macadam-izing Bloor Street", debating the virtues of oak chip and granite block. The demand to improve roads increased as more businesses incorporated automobiles and trucks into their operations. The Bell Telephone Company had purchased a car in 1909 to be used for telephone repairs, installing new lines and performing other development tasks. With time, they motorized all such operations. In 1914 an agreement had been reached between the provinces to spend sixty million dollars on roads. At that time a good macadam road cost between five and six thousand dollars a mile.

In 1833 a stretch of Yonge Street about one mile in length was the first to be macadamized in British North America. But techniques changed as the weather revealed the pressures it put on the road surfaces, and as the vehicles of transportation changed and their frequency of use increased. Deeply rutted mud roads had been frequently complained about in early settlement life. Initially, Toronto's roads had been primarily built with logs. The main trunk of the tree would be cut up in lengths of fifteen inches and sold to the road builder. Block pavement well laid made an excellent road. Four-by-eight timbers were used for curbs, placed at either side at the desired distance apart. The sand bed was dug to the desired depth and then rolled smooth with a steamroller. It was formed as a domed surface, graded slightly to either curb in order to let the water run off into grilled openings and through to the sewers. The wooden blocks were set on the hard-packed sand as closely as possible. Small gravel and sand was then laid on top of the blocks, tamped and soaked with oil. This made a very durable and quiet surface over which the horses and carriages tramped. I have watched many roads being made in this way.

As the trees became more scarce, other materials were sought out for road building. Concrete and crushed stone were laid between the curbs. This was done at varying depths, but one cold front could ruin the surface layer. Then came the excavation to a deeper level in order to lay thicker concrete as a base with a top surface of bitulithic and tar.

Road building has been refined and has progressed since that time culminating in the Queen Elizabeth Highway, which was the first illuminated highway in North America when it was completed.

The roads within Toronto were also improved and further organized. A semaphore system for signals at intersections was installed to help deal with the increased vehicle traffic in 1919.

Improved highways and the increased number of trucks on the road made it possible to institute the slogan "from producer to consumer" and make it fact. Unlike the railways from whom they now took over the business, trucks were not limited to providing service along pre-set routes which forced farmers to deliver their own goods over many miles from their farms to the nearest railway station. Truckers drove to the farmer's yard, helped load the goods and delivered them directly to the market and/or wholesalers to whom they were to be sold. It was the beginning of fierce competition between the two means of transport although in the early days of trucking, the railway owners did not see truckers as a threat.

With the obvious changes that the vehicle would bring to all of business life, Mr. Skeans was receptive to change. On one of their trips south, the Skeans had been to visit a brother in Los Angeles. There, they saw the impact of the automobile on life and the corresponding development and expansion of the chain-store idea for grocery sales. Mr. Skeans realized that his tea business, as part of the pedlar's type of operation, was bound to be affected. He knew how many of the householders' goods were delivered by pedlars and could see that the chain store would have a devastating effect on this business. So, he decided it would be timely to get rid of it. Up until that time, he had been converting most of his earnings into brick and mortar, keeping faith in Toronto's future. He bought up brick dwellings and stores and, with all his purchases, my work load increased since I was his rent collector. There was a man pressing him to sell out to him and his father, and this man was the bank manager with whom we dealt. The manager could see the daily receipts of the business as they came into the bank and from this he measured it as a successful business.

After discussing the deal with me and noting that my brother Cecil would soon be out of the army and looking for work, he suggested that I might want to take him on as a partner and take over the business myself. This I turned down. Cec was not a salesman and, with my game leg, I thought I would do better at something else.

Mr. Skeans had countless discussions with the purchaser and an agreement was finally made whereby I would remain working with the firm for one year in order to show the new owner the ins and outs of the business. When the year was over, I returned to working with my father-in-law.

Mr. Skeans, in the meantime, thought considerably about the wholesale tea and grocery business, but it was not a quick money-making venture. One needed a lot of merchandise; goods were only taken on consignment and paid for when sold. So, it entailed a lot of credit and outlay of cash. Mr. Skeans was hesitant about this practice as he had always been.

At this time, he was approached by Theodore Pringle Loblaw and Mr. Milton Cork to help them finance a self-serve, cash-and-carry grocery store, the precursor of today's large Loblaws chain. In 1900, Mr. Loblaw had opened his first store, which he built up and later sold as the basis of the present-day Dominion Stores. But Mr. Skeans turned down the opportunity although he believed in their concept. It was an idea for the future.

The two men's success was immediate and they decided to expand. Again, they needed capital for their venture and they approached Mr. Skeans with evidence of their success, their plans for future expansion as a limited company, with many more such grocery stores in Toronto, throughout the province, and even into the States. Once again, however, he turned down the chance.

In my courting days, my wife's family had lived next door to the LePage family on Thorold Avenue. I got to know the boys personally and Ed had said to me that if ever I thought of turning to real estate, he would like me to try him first. They were already doing well. But Mr. Skeans and I went into the real estate business together.

Somebody had five acres of land for sale on Salmon Avenue, part of a farm in the East York Township. It was cheap and Mr. Skeans and I bought it without knowing that the city had been unable to make a deal previously with the owner for the entire parcel of land. Farms all around it had been bought up, subdivided and developed. The city had tried, to no effect, to make the same deal with the farmer who owned this land, but he still farmed and cropped his land. In fact, he lived in the barn on his property and retained the one hundred acres around it to farm. When the town surveyors had come onto his property to survey it and to lay out the lines for sewers and streets for the future development, he had chased them off the property with his shotgun. We thought the city would win and so we waited. They wanted a site for a hospital and a school. The city had negotiated sufficient land for these purposes and they offered a solid price to the owner. They then put a perimeter boundary tax on the balance of the farm, including our land. Our taxes went up five times over the original price and eventually we traded the land and the farmer left. We had laid out the streets and planned a mass production of houses for rental. We had even named one of the streets after daughter June. We suffered a considerable loss on the deal and over the years, although I was offered many opportunities in land speculation, I was always leery because of this bad experience.

For the sale of the properties we had leased a store on Danforth Avenue. For two years we worked at selling land, but the market had gone soft. Food prices were high in Toronto, wages were low and, although there was a housing shortage, people couldn't afford to buy.

While I was sitting around waiting for things to happen, an insurance company representative came in and talked about setting up an insurance office. He suggested to me that it might be more profitable to work at selling insurance than to wait around for real estate to develop.

So, I started into my final business, insurance. I apprenticed through the company of Mitchell and Ryerson in the beginning and later started up on my own. Perhaps one didn't need as much knowledge in the early days of the industry. It was a relatively new field, not nearly so widespread as it is now. Many retired people sold insurance part-time because it was a growing industry. I had had years of canvassing sales, so I thought it would be a cinch! First off, I rang doorbells for one full day and didn't get any business.

The next day, I tried a little different approach and enjoyed a few nibbles. I introduced the wives to the idea during the day and then returned in the evening to see the husbands after their wives had talked to them. This did bring results. One day, during the day, I encountered the gentleman of the house immediately and thought it was a good opportunity to save myself a return trip. I asked him whether or not he had any insurance on his property and he said, "No I don't need any because God will protect me from fire!"

I asked him quietly, then, why he had shingles

on the roof or fire in the furnace during the winter. "Surely God will protect you from cold as He does from fire?" I suggested.

He slammed the door in my face! It just goes to show that there are many different types of people in the world.

I kept at the insurance business for sixty years and retired for the benefit of my son who took over the business when I was eighty.

In the early days, you had to follow any lead you got and trust to your ability to harvest what was at the end of the rainbow. I worked along with the car salesman, Curly Clements. When he sold a car to someone, I would try to sell them the insurance. Growth in both sales was encouraging.

One day Curly sold a Chevrolet car to a Jack Richardson on Hamilton Street. I drove down to Hamilton Street in my Ford and called on him to suggest insuring his new car. Jack was not at home when I called but he was due back at any moment according to his wife. While we waited, I talked to Mrs. Richardson. She thought the liability insurance was a good idea and so did Jack when he came into the house. Then, I found out that Jack owned a small truck for hauling groceries. I emphasized to him that by insuring two or more vehicles with me he would be able to get a fifteen percent discount.

Jack thought about this and suggested, "I have a young friend who works for the same wholesale grocery house that I work for and I don't think he has any insurance either. Could he insure along with me and get the same discount?"

I agreed. In the early days with competition for the business, this was allowed, so I wrote the business and financed it myself.

The young friend's name was George Rodanz. I also sold him a one-thousand-dollar load insurance policy. One day his truck caught fire with a load of groceries aboard. His load was from the Great Atlantic and Pacific Tea Company, now known as the A&P. Since load insurance was a new thing in those days, not at all a standard practice as it is now, A&P assumed they had sustained a loss.

When I went to the insurance company for payment of the claim, I gave them the names of both A&P and George Rodanz. I took the cheque over to Rodanz and had him endorse it right then and there. The cheque for a truckload of groceries was for seven hundred and ninety dollars and I took it over to A&P immediately. They were so happy that they made a decision that anybody hauling for them should insure with me. Consequently, I reaped quite a harvest of new business.

Through the careful payment of every honest claim in the early days of the business, I got into the truck transport business. It was growing and a good one in which to be involved. Many success stories started small in the trucking business and later expanded. A&P had a hand in many such stories.

George Rodanz was involved in yet another of these. He had started his own local cartage company in 1926 with one vehicle. Originally, he had been a milk collector and a farmer. Then A&P hired him and were so pleased with the service he provided their Toronto store that, when they opened a store in Brampton, they hired him to do the cartage. Naturally, he had to buy another truck, and with this as impetus he started Direct Transport, which later became Direct Transportation. This is one of the largest trucking businesses in operation in Canada today and it is still operated by one of George Rodanz' sons.

In those days, you looked out for the welfare of your customer. You kept your eyes and ears open. One of my transport customers was more of a dealer than a truck man. He put his few trucks and their routes up for sale. The purchaser happened to be a friend of mine. The night before the delivery of the equipment, the seller had his men substitute a number of worn tires on the trucks, taking off newer, better ones to do it. The word got to me about this and, of course, I let the purchaser know. He was a former policeman. He had the seller change back to good tires and was very grateful to me, because it was worth about nine hundred dollars to him. I kept his business for over forty years.

It took me about four years to get established in the fire and casualty insurance business. All that time I rang doorbells and canvassed myself, experiencing many adventures. In those days, house and furniture insurance was carried for three years. When the fourth year came around and the renewals came in, the ship was launched and I never looked back.

I ran the business from the third-floor front room of our home on Boustead Avenue. My desk was at the window. On one very fine day, the family had decided to go out for a ride but, having work to do, I remained behind. I watched the car leave the driveway and knew that I was alone in the house. But the silence was broken, when I heard a thud followed by a vibration.

There was not any carpet on the attic staircase, and I was wearing heavy army-issue boots so I could not creep down the stairs quietly to investigate. Instead, I charged down the uncarpeted stairs two at a time, then down the carpeted ones as fast as I could to the short hall with doors on each end to the kitchen. The front door in the short hall was swinging ajar when I went through it on the run. The latch door to the kitchen slammed in my face. I knew it was the pressure on the first door that had caused the kitchen door to close so hard. I put my hand up to my hair and it was standing on end. So, it was no myth!

I discovered that the burglars had endeavoured to spring open the storm door into the dining room off the small verandah, but luckily that trick didn't work. That same afternoon, our neighbours over the back fence were burglarized and lost all of their silver. They were not insured and they suffered a considerable loss.

For some years one of the more pleasant features of the street railway service had been the Belt Line, a ride along Bloor Street, down Sherbourne, back along King Street and up Spadina to Bloor again. In the first year of its service, a horse had provided the power; in the next year, the streetcar had been powered by electricity.

In warm weather young blades had taken their sweethearts for a toot on the loops. Older folks had taken the cooler breezes offered by the ride as the sun went down. Mothers and fathers with their children bought tickets at ten for a quarter for children. Adults paid five cents for a ride. My wife, Ruby, had then been my sweetheart and we had enjoyed the ride many times.

After dark, we had watched for the red and yellow or green and blue drugstore lights and the other city sights that we loved . . . the peanut and popcorn cart with its small tin whistle and hissing flare, the cigar stores with their carved wooden Indians standing outside, advertising the sale of tobacco. This latter tradition was popular in Toronto

Howard House (Colborne Lodge) — High Park — 1836

until the fifties or sixties. By then, the Belt Line had long since faded into memory. Open streetcars — a favourite feature of the Belt Line — were banned in 1915.

Industry, automobiles and electricity were changing the city radically. Slowly it became better organized. It was around 1915 that a problem that had long plagued city engineers was solved. Bloor Street had always been a particularly important and busy one. Even today, it extends westward beyond the western limits of the city. But, crossing Keele Street then, Bloor had climbed a steep hill to the high land of the northern boundary of High, or Howard Park as it was then known. Then the dip in the road west of there was a dandy — right down to lake level at Grenadier Pond. This dip was Bloor Street's biggest problem, one which had to be solved to cope with the increasing traffic. A bridge was out of the question because there were streets running north with which Bloor Street had to connect. Minutes from the City Council meetings indicate that long discussions were held about this problem and many studies were commissioned to attempt to find a solution.

Finally, the decision was made to fill in this deep depression by building a long trestle about sixty feet above lake level. The engineers determined the level, built the trestle, suspended the sewers, water and gas mains and all the other requirements from the top trestle beams. Then they laid a rail along the top and ran small dump cars along it with the necessary fill material. Massive amounts of fill were necessary to completely bury the trestle and bring the street up to its present level.

After the fill had settled, the top surface was laid with roadbuilding materials and a car track was put down for the streetcar. Glendonwynne Avenue was graded up to meet the Bloor level. This levelling opened up the entire Runnymede area of the city, north of Swansea, and made Bloor a continuous street all the way out and over the Humber River. A new bridge was built over the Humber. A flume was built to carry the water from the Kennedy duck pond and stream to Grenadier Pond. The natural flow of the water had been blocked by the sinking of the trestle and the fill of the road.

On the northeast side of the Bloor Street fill the gracious old residence of Dr. McCormick stood. Part way down the hill, a spring gave off a small stream of water. When this water was tested, it gave off a mineral smell. Dr. McCormick had built a small bathing pool which he advertised as the Mineral Baths. This was not affected by the fill. A friend of mine, Harvey Hamilton, was the first lifeguard at this pool.

Sometimes in this era the city seemed to be changing overnight in front of our wondering eyes. In the 1920s we could still hear the cocks crowing when we awoke on Sunday mornings to go off to church. People kept chickens, pigeons and rabbits in their back yards. Butchers had their own small stores. Loblaws, Dominion and the A&P had several grocery stores in the city, based on the cash-and-carry principle. Simpsons and Eaton's still delivered their customers' goods by horse and wagon as did the Mountain Tea Blend Company, but cars and trucks were becoming the more commonly used form of transport. Traffic was increasing daily. Streets were being paved throughout the city. There was money to be made for those willing to work hard, but housing had not kept pace with the demands nor had public transportation. The city's limits had expanded outwards to accommodate the growing number of people who immigrated to the city to work. Many people had to travel long distances to their places of work and they demanded increased and improved transportation.

Public expectations had been changed with the presence of some persuasive politicians such as Adam Beck. In the first years of the twentieth century he had rallied the people of Ontario to insist that the government harness the potential electrical power of Niagara Falls rather than allow it to be monopolized by a few individuals. They had won the battle and the legislation to form the Hydro-Electric Power Commission of Ontario (now known as Hydro), the world's first publicly owned utility, was drawn up in 1906. With this success, the way was paved for further changes.

The Toronto Street Railway was owned and operated by many of the same men who had sought to monopolize distribution of electricity. Since the huge streetcar fire in 1916 at the King Street garage, their company had been unable or unwilling to spend the capital to provide the necessary extensions and more modern vehicles. Service was deteriorating and the public was pressuring the city government to take over the service. In 1920, the Toronto Transportation Commission was formed and it took over operations of the system the following year, instituting a pay-as-you-pass collection system of fares. New cars were ordered by the TTC immediately — the now famous Peter Witt cars. These were painted bright red to replace the drab chocolate brown and green colour of the lines they had taken over. This helped the public to identify with their newly unified system. New, wider track was laid. A systematic modernization was undertaken for the entire operation. In the next few years underpasses were constructed on Bloor Street; the ferry service to the island was taken over and improved; lines were extended into the suburbs, with buses and trolleys used as feeders and commuters to the main street-cars in the city's core areas. A bathing car service was instituted which carried children free to Sunnyside Beach or Ferry Docks in the summer months. Service was extended to Long Branch, Mimico Beach and points west.

In 1921, an American corporation had established the consumer credit corporation, a major new invention to encourage the purchase of new cars with high-interest loans. The city bought snow-removal equipment. Dr. Archie McCallum joined the Canadian Navy and served for three years before retiring to private practice until the next war, when he would be called upon again to serve his country.

Andrew Carnegie, an American philanthropist, had donated money to the city to build and stock a library at the beginning of the century. The public library had opened its doors to an interested and growing public and more branches had been opened up throughout the city.

The Toronto Grade Separation elevated railway tracks along the waterfront and protected the shoreline. Queen's Quay, Fleet Street and other roadways were constructed.

Mines throughout the province were opened up, many of them with Toronto money, increasing the prosperity of some of her citizens, encouraging their speculation. The forest was being similarly productive as a field of industry, speculation and profit.

Always a man of strong individual ideals, my brother Al decided to give up his career in chemical engineering in 1922 to devote himself to teaching the young people of the city, particularly the girls, how to swim and dive. The first place at which he gave these lessons was at Dr. McCormick's Mineral Baths. His objective was to teach the youth to swim and dive, not to make money. All he wanted was enough to pay for the pool they used during the classes.

He formed the High Park Diving Club first and the girls got much of their practice plunging from the diving tower out at the Mineral Baths. This stood them in good stead later at the Canadian Diving Championships and still later at the Olympics. Dr. McCormick had known Alex well, and his lifeguard, Hamilton, was a good friend.

Things were not particularly organized in Al's club with a secretary, treasurer and president. It was his own club and his objective was to provide leadership and training. Friends from the YMCA, such as Ed Archibald, Ardagh Scythes, Jack Tate and Bill Messing, supported his work. Eventually, he approached Hart House and rented its pool and then, with the help of his friends from the "Y" he approached the Board of Education and pointed out that several of the high schools had excellent pools standing idle much of the time. The board suggested that these pools be put to use by the club.

When Jarvis Collegiate accepted this proposal and made its facilities available, Al formed the Dolphinets in 1927. This became his permanent base. From their beginnings, the Dolphinets had an impact on the diving and swimming competitions across Canada. From 1929 until 1951, and with few exceptions in between, all Canadian Diving Champions were Dolphinets. Al also developed something he called ornamental swimming and the girls gave very popular demonstrations in Toronto and even in the US. Coaches there were so impressed with this activity that they later developed synchronized swimming, a field in which Al did much of the pioneer work, although his efforts have largely been unrecognized.

Al paid seven dollars and fifty cents each day the pool was used and he charged each girl twenty-five cents for her attendance at each class. From 6 to 7 p.m. there would be a free swim with no instruction and then for the next two hours there were classes and training. If the girls didn't have the necessary quarter, they were allowed to participate anyway.

Al was a kind but stern trainer and he got results. Girls were urged to repeat a dive again and again until they got it right according to Al's demanding expectations. Al was the official coach for the 1934 team that went to the British Empire Games and also for the team that went to the 1936 Berlin Olympics. Some of the names of girls remembered for their achievements in the field and whom Al coached included Doris Ogilvie, Thelma Brigham, Evelyn Buchan and Irene Pirie. At one time Irene Pirie held every woman's record from fifty yards to one mile. Alex devoted all his energies to this task and died quite penniless. His contribution was recognized by the city, however, in the large funeral given to him. More important, a permanent memorial, the first Olympic-sized pool in the city at Christie Pits, was named after him — the Alex Duff Memorial Pool.

During this period of rapid growth and change, city folk needed a place to let off steam. Lol Solomon ran

Sunnyside Amusement Park — 1920-1943

the Sunnyside Amusement Park at the foot of Roncesvalles Avenue, then called Sunnyside Beach, as well as the park at Hanlan's Point where the huge roller coasters, Ferris wheels and shooting galleries always seemed to be in full swing. The chant of the ring-toss men "throw them high, drop them low, over the cane they are bound to go" was a popular one, providing hours of entertainment at three rings for only a quarter. If you did manage to throw the ring over the cane, you walked home with it under your arm. This amusement park was enjoyed until the building of the Gardiner Expressway forced it to be demolished in the fifties.

With the expanding population, housing, sanitation, working conditions and health facilities had not been able to keep pace. Some parts of Toronto suffered appalling poverty, particularly her crowded core. There was little organized help to deal with this social illness.

In 1882 the Salvation Army had come to Canada and held its first informal meetings. Several years later, Toronto's first official Army captain from England, Susan James, came to begin rescue work among the fallen women of Toronto. In the ensuing years the Army founded rescue missions, homes for ex-prisoners, and soup kitchens. Their lively parades and street-corner musical meetings became part of the early life of the city. Their building at 20 Albert Street is at the same site as their earliest building.

In 1885 the Sisters of the St. John the Divine, an Anglican order of nuns, the first in Canada, was founded by Mother Hannah Grier Coome in Toronto. First recognized for their nursing of soldiers in the North-West Rebellion of 1885, they opened mission houses, provided shelter for the aged and infirm, established hospitals and served meals to the destitute. The nuns worked in the area of the church of St. Stephen-in-the-Fields, around the Kensington Market, an area of immigration and change, at that time largely populated by Jews who worked in the "sweatshops" in the Spadina district.

The Salvation Army and the Sisters of St. John the Divine were the basis of social service in Toronto.

As immigrants had arrived from all over the world, Toronto the Good, Anglo-Saxon to the core, was changed visibly. The old families continued to wield power with their wealth, but this was being challenged and often changed with time. There were labour unrest and strikes. Eventually, some laws were enacted giving workers some rights, entitling them to shorter working hours, higher pay and better working conditions.

As the city's population grew to include other nationalities, its strong puritanical strain was countered by other equally powerful religious and social beliefs. Beer was a part of many workingmen's daily lives, and even the presence of such forces as the WCTU, the Salvation Army and others could not alter these attitudes.

Women had been active in securing the vote for themselves and a greater recognition of their rights as individuals, not as pawns of their husbands or the state. They had been active in promoting prohibition. For many years my sister, Rosamond, worked for the Women's Christian Temperance Union as its secretary; both my mother and my Aunt Elizabeth had been active for that cause. They viewed liquor as the chief cause of brutality toward women, the abuse of children and other social ills. My Grandfather Richey, whose own grandson had been a victim of strong drink, had thrown all spirits out of his home and declared it a temperance house. I can remember many meetings of the WCTU being held in our home.

The Anglican Church had lost its sway over the city as Toronto's population became more diverse. Part of this was also due, no doubt, to the separation of school and church. Education became available for everyone in public schools. The formation of the United Church in Canada, when the majority of Presbyterian, Methodist, Council of Local Union Churches and Congregational churches joined forces in 1925, was also significant. The inauguration of the new church was celebrated in a massive service at the Mutual Street Arena. Church property was assessed and resources were pooled to form the new church. Some of its well-known adherents included Sir Robert Falconer, University of Toronto, N.W. Rowell, one-time leader of the provincial Liberals, Egerton Ryerson and other familiar names.

Both women's groups and many of the churches advocated social change — the creation of unemployment insurance, old age pensions and other social benefits for the less privileged and for those who fell on hard times.

Reverend James Edward Ward, rector of St. Stephen-in-the-Fields, pioneered religious radio broadcasts in 1927. This broadened the range of his parish and was the precursor of a trend in religious broadcasting that spread to lengths never imagined by him.

But by 1926 the prices of food and goods were dropping with the increasing prosperity of the city and few people seemed to consider the needs of those with less than they had. Over six hundred thousand people lived in Toronto. There was a feeling of optimism. A telephone cost two dollars and forty cents monthly. Trucking fleets were responsible for shipping the majority of farmer's produce in the province. Competition between the railways and the trucking industry became marked. The railway had federal government support, but the truckers were able to provide cheaper, more efficient service and they were supported by the merchants, wholesalers and farmers.

In 1928 Toronto Elevators Ltd. opened a concrete building on the waterfront for the storage of grain prior to shipping, opening up the city as a centre for grain shipping by truck, train and ship. Loblaws built a new head office and warehouse at Lakeshore Boulevard and Bathurst where coffee, mayonnaise and candy were processed and manufactured and baked goods were made. Their own brand goods were distributed from the same location.

The city had replaced most of its wooden block streets to make way for the automobile. Traffic lights replaced the old-fashioned semaphore system for traffic control. The Liquor Control Board of Ontario opened government liquor stores throughout the province. Districts that voted to remain dry, however, continued to do so. A large tax benefit accrued immediately to the province from the sales. The Ontario Research Foundation was established in Toronto and Banting and Best were funded to conduct their research into diabetes. Finally, the provincial government instituted old age pensions in cooperation with the federal government which had been pushing the issue for some time. However, these were only for people over seventy who passed a strict means test!

Then came Black Thursday, October 24, 1929 — the crash of the stock markets and financial institutions all across North America. People lost their fortunes overnight; many of them plunged out of top-floor windows to commit suicide. Henry Pellatt lost Casa Loma to the city for back taxes. We were lucky and I managed to maintain our business throughout those black days.

As fortunes dwindled to nothing and as prairie farmers faced the worst drought in history, the welfare lines, the soup lines, the lines of jobless and hopeless grew. There were few organizations and institutions to provide the necessary support and assistance and what they did seemed inadequate compared to the enormity of the task. In times past, charity had been a moral responsibility for the rich to provide, but as the rich themselves were undermined, many people too proud to seek help suffered.

Men who had banded together to help each other in workmen's guilds and other service organizations — the Masons, the Independent Order of Foresters, the Kiwanis and the Kinsmen, to mention just a few — did what they could for their members and others. Some individuals who were more fortunate than others rallied to provide what help they could muster.

Rodger Leslie and the Leslie family were such individuals. R.R. Leslie had started his own trucking company, Canada Cartage, back in 1914. It had expanded and prospered and was then being run by Rodger Leslie, his son. R.R. had gone on to become a city alderman, a position he held for many years. When the Depression was at its worst, the entire Leslie family was mobilized to help. R.R. Leslie made a deal to pay a very modest rent on an empty store on Queen, just east of Crawford Street. There, he established a large soup kitchen where the entire family daily served more than a hundred people with a hot meal of soup, plenty of bread and butter and steaming coffee. The family did the cooking and served the sit-down meal to whomever came to the soup kitchen. At Christmastime the dining room was festooned with cheer for the season, brightened by the Leslies' spirit.

As the project became properly established, companies came to the Leslie family's assistance. Both Swifts and Canada Packers donated meat; Ideal Bakeries donated bread; other companies within the district and throughout the city made donations. It was an excellent example of private initiative helping to alleviate a social ill, something which is seldom seen today now that there are welfare and other forms of social assistance provided by the state. On more than one occasion the Leslies proved their generosity of spirit, their kind of caring for their fellow men as a later incident will exemplify. The Leslie family's soup kitchen fed people throughout the winter of 1931 to 1932 and was finally closed when the need for its service seemed to have lessened.

In 1932, with some of the confidence restored in the market in merchandising and manufacturing, I was invited to join the West Toronto Kiwanis Club. The first thing the club did on the day that I joined was to give me a surprise baby shower. My youngest child, my second daughter, had been born that day. Ruby and I already had one daughter and a son. It was a day of tremendous excitement and they certainly did help me celebrate the occasion in a memorable fashion.

Initially, the group had been formed as a means of helping each other. Accordingly, only two representatives of each kind of business or professional life — that is, two insurance salesmen, two dentists, two greengrocers — could be a part of each club so that the group could provide a cross-section of

King Street looking west
from Jarvis Street —
1933

business and professional people. Our motto was "we build".

There was still considerable poverty in the city with people running out of money and work and too proud to ask for help. (To be considered for welfare, men had to surrender their liquor permit, their licence plate and driver's licence. It was a depressing process which left no dignity to those forced to apply for benefits.) Some of the more fortunate members of society wanted to find a means of helping and many of us chose to join clubs such as the Kiwanis (an idea imported from Chicago in 1924). As a group, we were often able to render assistance which we could not extend as individuals. We were particularly interested in the youth of Toronto. One of our earliest and most rewarding efforts was the creation of a Boys' Camp on the Credit River by the town of Claireville. We had a contractor and a builder in the club and we touched all the members and their friends for the cash to buy the essential materials.

Every member who could swing a hammer or use a saw got involved in the fun. We built two sleeping cabins, a kitchen and eating quarters. We obtained permission from the authorities to build a log dam which created a good swimming hole. During the season, it was supervised by the YMCA. Our contribution to boys' work was swept away by Hurricane Hazel in 1954, but while it was still in operation and during the season it paid enormous dividends in pleasure.

When the Claireville Camp was organized, we went head over heels into the operation of Casa Loma. The city had taken it over for back taxes in 1929 but was bewildered as to what to do with it. Fortunately, Bill Bothwell, one of our forward-thinking members, was listening to a radio program one day on which Claire Wallace told a tale of getting permission from the city to spend a night in this haunted castle. The yarn was descriptive and very interesting to a Kiwanis member looking for ways to make money for our charitable activities.

A club meeting was called, the idea proposed and accepted, and we formed a committee to deal with the city. Very shortly, a deal was worked out that we would clean up the interior, the city would take care of the exterior, and we would give twenty-five percent of all gate receipts to the city on a long-term basis.

Even while we were working toward the clean-up and opening of our new facility, Sir Henry paid our club a visit and addressed us. Although his earlier dream had not materialized, he expressed happiness that his efforts and ours would be used for charitable purposes.

The conversion of Casa Loma into the major tourist attraction that it is today, took a lot of coordinated effort and a lot of elbow grease. Seven hundred glass lights had to be replaced, a nesting bird population had to be chased out and evidence of their habitation removed. Heavy street brushes had to be used to clean out the manure and shovels to clear away the piles of dirt and other accumulation. Then, everything had to be painted, scrubbed, stripped and generally brightened up for visitors. Finally, we opened to the public on May 24, 1937. The Eaton Company had loaned us yards and yards of bunting, plates, medallions and numerous flags to brighten the premises on the day of opening to our first visitors. We put over one hundred and twenty thousand people through the place in the first year.

Over the years, Casa Loma has more than repaid the city for the deal which they made with us, providing the city with more money than any comparable buildings on the site would have done from tax revenue.

When dancing was at its height in the city during the forties and early fifties, top bands played at the castle drawing huge crowds. The beautiful Wurlitzer organ that was used at Shea's Theatre on Bay Street had been picked up at the demolition of the building by one of our friends, Mr. Connie Smythe. Initially, he had no place to put it but simply did not wish to see it demolished. When the castle was turned over to the Kiwanis on a long-term lease, he turned the organ over to the club. It was installed in the castle by the Ontario Organists' Association at no charge. Its presence has greatly augmented an already successful tourist venture. Casa Loma is a proud and unusual landmark for our city today.

But historic consequences of this era had not all been positive and between the depression and the declaration of the Second World War, Toronto's progress as a city was irregular.

Many public works programs had been instituted to improve roads and to modernize the streetcars and the tracks of the TTC, as part of the public's make-work projects during the depression. Labour had suffered greatly from unemployment and unions had gained strength. A forty-hour week had been instituted, a minimum wage established and higher wages granted to workers. C.G. McCullough had purchased the *Toronto Globe* and the *Mail* and merged the two papers to form the now nationally known Toronto *Globe and Mail*. He had made his money from gold in Ontario's north. Fort York had been restored and opened to the public to celebrate the city's one hundredth birthday. Both of my in-laws, the Skeans, had died and Ruby and I had begun to build our own home in Etobicoke. We had three beautiful children — two daughters and a son.

It was a sobered city which faced the Second World War in 1939.

Jesse Ashbridge Home — overlooking Ashbridge's Bay — 1854

St. Lawrence Weigh Scales — Front and Jarvis Streets — 1873-1964

Rosedale Ravine — Sherbourne Street Bridge — 1890

Gamble's Grist Mill — The Old Mill — Humber River — 1850

CHAPTER FIVE

The Last Forty Years

Our family grew up with Toronto and when the Second World War broke out we all had young and growing families. Just prior to its outbreak, I had designed and built a house for the Skeans, Ruby and me and our three children. The new house was built on Riverside Drive, along the edge of the Humber River. It was a twelve-room house with a billiard room containing a full-sized table and a table for ping pong. We still lived with my wife's parents. Households were extended in those days; there were few old age homes and many members of the same family and different generations lived together in larger houses. Our living arrangements were typical.

For over thirty years of our married life we employed the same wash lady, Mrs. Wilson, and, while she was with us, we enjoyed the advent of the electric mangle. This was an important breakthrough in household appliances because washing day was still a long and heavy one. Sheets and table cloths were routinely sent out to commercial laundries. Paper napkins and other such modern labour-saving inventions had not yet been put onto the market. With the purchase of our electric mangle, however, our household became more self-sufficient because we were able to launder our own sheets and table cloths properly.

No member of our family served on the battle-grounds of Europe in World War Two. Rosamond, who had remained in our old family home, continued her work with CCM and the WCTU, for whom she worked in the field services. My twin sisters, Jay and Lillian, were also working. Jay, who had operated as a legal secretary before her marriage, raised three boys and returned to the same firm after twenty years when her husband died. Lillian held only one job in her life. She worked in the Mother's Allowance Department of the Ontario Government, cycling to work daily unless weather prevented it. Lillian knew every inch of the department in which she worked but, because she was a woman, she was never promoted to the position of commissioner.

Toronto sacrificed many of her young sons to the Second World War as she had done to the first. I continued to work in the insurance field in the city, still ineligible for service. Besides the loss of life and property resulting from the conflict, social and technical changes resulted that were far reaching. Many of these changes I witnessed firsthand. It was only after the Second World War that Toronto grew into a major city.

Bickering between the trucking industry and the railways was temporarily halted. Everybody's efforts had to be directed toward a united front as must happen in times of war and natural disaster. Trucks became travelling billboards carrying advertising for Victory War Bonds and other messages of support for the war effort. In my childhood the trains had carried the weather broadcasts; perhaps this was a sign of the times in itself.

Labatt's Brewery trucks became the good guys on the road, stopping to help other motorists in trouble. By the end of the war these and other efforts had caused much of the bad feeling about trucks and truckers to be forgotten and forgiven. The first pneumatic tires developed had had an extremely high psi and were very high priced. Whenever these tires blew, everyone in the town would jump! Springs had been rigid, trucks heavy and motors worn out by twenty-five thousand miles of travel. Speed was slow and ponderous. Research and development, as always fuelled by the war's needs, changed all of this and the modern tractor-trailer truck, capable of obtaining high speeds and travelling thousands of miles without a complete overhaul, became common on the ever-expanding highways.

There was an increased demand for public transit because gas, oil and rubber were needed for the war and made private automobiles a low priority. The trolley was king. Women were employed as motormen and conductors.

Dr. Archie McCallum, our friend from the OCTO LAETE days, was called on by the government for help. He joined the navy and organized naval medical services from Halifax. In recognition of his important work he became Surgeon Commander, the first man in the medical branch of the Canadian Services to achieve such a rank.

The government passed the Vacations with Pay Act limiting hours of work in a week and guaranteeing a yearly holiday for regular salaried employees. Unemployment insurance was instituted after much pressure from women's groups, the church and the newly formed government party of the CCF.

When men returned to their own country to work after the war, Toronto became more crowded. Office space was at a premium, as was housing, because no new houses nor offices had been built during the war, and few had been built during the

depression prior to it. Once again, the highways and streets became crowded with private cars and trucks. Bloor Street and Yonge Street, particularly, became jammed, and in 1946 a plebiscite was held to consider the idea of the urban subway system which had first been suggested in 1911. It was popularly endorsed and digging was begun in 1949.

With the resumption of manufacture, the harbour again became the focus of attention. In 1937 the airport for both light aircraft and seaplanes had opened at the southwest corner of Toronto Island and was operated by the Toronto Harbour Commission.

During the war, large destroyers had become a part of the Canadian Navy's operations, some of which were retired to our Toronto harbour after the war. The *Haida* was one of these. It was one of the most notable ships built by P. Vickers and Armstrong Company of Newcastle-on-Tyne when it was delivered in 1943. Other Canadian ships in the same class were the *Iroquois*, the *Huron* and the *Athabaskan*. The *Athabaskan* was lost in combat. These ships were particularly fast, running at over forty miles per hour. Responsible for keeping the channels and the convoys free from attack, they were equipped with two four-inch guns with a nine-mile range. The *Haida* was later used in the Korean War to patrol the coastline of Korea. She is now permanently anchored beside Ontario Place where the public may tour her decks.

The plan to build the Seaway instituted important forward thinking and planning for the Toronto harbourfront, even before the concept had been agreed upon by both Canadian and American governments. The harbour had to be dredged to a depth of twenty-seven feet to accommodate sea-going vessels; the Turning Basin was also designed to accommodate these larger vessels. Good anchorage was needed for oil tankers and grain boats, plus machinery for loading and unloading them. In fact, plenty of back yard and a railway track are essential for shipping concerns. Studies were made and warehouses and terminals were planned and built. New equipment was acquired to accommodate the increased demands foreseen for the waterfront facilities.

The harbour, east of Yonge Street from Parliament to Leslie, had a swampy shoreline unsuitable for bathing or even boating of any sort. Cherry Street with its lift bridge provided the city with good access to the large sand bar here and its slowly developing commercial area. The Don River emptied into the bay through Keating's Channel which was kept dredged to allow the free flow of the river's water into the lake.

Construction of the many downtown buildings and the subway made a local site for dumping essential. The site chosen for this fill was the foot of Leslie Street. Continuous dumping of the heavy clay and slate excavated from the downtown projects was used to create a foundation for this new parcel of land which is called an Aquatic Park, a refuge for thousands of birds. It protects the outer harbour, making safe anchorage possible if necessary. It also protects the new Eastern Gap from stormy weather. When this newly created land is properly landscaped it will give Toronto acres more recreational and functional park land, garden and beauty.

The land that has been reclaimed to create the extension of Cherry Street is now a major industrial area. Over eighty percent of the incoming shipments at the waterfront are reshipped by transport companies to manufacturing locations in Toronto, the rest of Ontario and many other parts of Canada. This has aided the trucking industry here greatly. As well, both the CNR and the CPR transcontinental railways serve this entire shipping area. Both railways had by then acquired trucking outfits and were competing in the business themselves. The shipping facilities are used less for foodstuffs than they are for commercial materials, such as oil, chemicals and machinery from the rest of the world.

The Harbour Life Saving Service was expanded to serve the area from Etobicoke to Scarborough, forming a vital link in the constantly increasing harbour life, both recreational and commercial.

With the change in mode of transportation from ship and rail to trucking for foodstuffs, the wholesale activity, which had been south of St. James' Cathedral and around the St. Lawrence Market for many years, was moved outside the city where a special terminal was constructed with government assistance. Prior to this, government assistance had been confined to the railways. The older area of the city had become congested as the trucks became larger and more numerous. The development of the refrigerator truck has made truck transport even more valuable in shipping perishable goods, such as fruits and vegetables.

After the war many boats were retired and sold for salvage. The *S.S. Toronto* was one of these. I had sold some insurance to the purchaser and, because he knew I was building a summer home at the time, he suggested that he might have something I could use in what he was selling. He invited me to come down to the wharf to take a look. I was curious enough to accept his invitation and down I went. I drove over the Cherry Street Bridge to the Turning Basin in the canal to meet him. On board there was some heavy mirror glass which I could use for bedroom mirrors, so I picked up some of that. I was turning to go when I saw a pair of metal lamps, one green and the other red. When I asked him casually, "What in the world are these?" he replied that they were the running lights from port and starboard of the *S.S. Toronto*. The lamps had used whale oil for fuel, a heavier oil, which could withstand the waves' pounding and still stay lit. We were already well into the electrical age by then and, although they needed repair, I was keen to have them. For only six dollars I bought the pair! Forty years later, after I had enjoyed the lamps as decoration at my cottage, I donated them to the Marine Museum, a proud symbol of Toronto's harbour heritage.

The Canada Steamship Line used to run many cruise ships in and out of the Toronto harbour for pleasure. They offered the people of Detroit and Cleveland a wonderful cruise to the Thousand Islands in the east end of Lake Ontario. In 1949 it was a nice autumn for sailing and the passenger agencies in Detroit and Chicago had no trouble in filling the available rooms. The sailing list numbered five hundred and twenty-four when the *S.S. Noronic* set out on her fatal cruise. She went through Lake Erie, through the Welland Canal, down one hundred and forty feet in stages to Lake Ontario with an overnight stop scheduled in Toronto harbour.

At two-thirty in the morning of September 17, 1949, the Toronto Fire Department got a call telling them that the steamer, the *S.S. Noronic*, was on fire. Nobody ever determined just where or how the fire started. The conjecture is that it started inside a linen cupboard and that the ship's crew had used fire extinguishers in an attempt to contain it, but had failed. By the time the Fire Department arrived, the entire ship was afire. There were no bulkheads nor fire doors anywhere on the ship to prevent the fire from travelling. Nobody had ever thought such a catastrophe would happen.

The Toronto Harbour Fire Boat assisted the Fire Department in fighting the blaze. With their combined efforts they were able to control the fire in two hours; but firemen couldn't get aboard the ship until seven o'clock the next morning because the ship was "white hot and the metal was buckled", according to the Fire Department's report. The *Kingston* and *Cayuga*, also passenger ships, were docked close by at the time but neither of them was damaged by the blaze. The pier to which the *Noronic* was docked had been ablaze when the firemen arrived but they had managed to save it with a minimum of damage.

Passengers did not fare as well. Many of them had been caught in bed without warning and had no time to flee for safety. Police, merchant sailors and civilians helped the firemen in the rescue of those passengers who leaped from the blazing ship into the icy waters of Lake Ontario. The onlookers watched and listened in horror, too often unable to help. The dead totalled one hundred and nineteen, mostly passengers. It was a dark day for the Toronto harbourfront, one which took many years to forget. It was September 17, 1949. A few years earlier, the *Noronic*'s sister ship, the *Hamonic*, had also been destroyed by fire with great loss of life.

But Toronto's harbour did have a cheerier side. More and more Torontonians were becoming sailors for pleasure. The Royal Canadian Yacht Club, now located on the Island, had formed a Junior Club to give sailing lessons. The *Hiawatha*, built in the late nineteenth century, a beautiful sixty-five-foot yacht with brass fittings, bells and gongs, was used to carry passengers to the club then as now. Recently, more yacht clubs have been formed, boat building has enjoyed a resurgence as an industry in Toronto, and the city has become one of the main yachting cities on the Great Lakes.

In the early 1920s and 1930s, Muskoka had become the summer place for Toronto people with money to buy some land. Four or five steamers plied the lakes taking passengers to this popular retreat. The *Medora* and the *Segwun* were among these craft. They were small and beautifully outfitted. Passengers would travel to Gravenhurst from the city by train, stay overnight on the train at their first stop and then board the cruiser early the next day. This was the popular one-hundred-mile cruise in my young adult days. There were no sleeping accommodations aboard these craft but tasty, wholesome and hearty meals were served.

Our good old friend, Charlie Musgrave, played the piano on the *Medora* for all of these years. He was a popular Toronto musician and he also ran a music shop in the old Yonge Street Arcade. He spent the summer months reciting the Indian lore of the early Muskoka area to the delight of the passengers. He was quite a storyteller.

My family — the Skeans, Ruby and I and the children — began to make our own excursions to the Muskoka area in the thirties, travelling by car to Gravenhurst and from there being picked up by friends to travel to their cottage site. The site on which we later built was known as Barlochan, home site of the Scottish Smith family who had farmed the area for the one hundred years before our arrival.

At that time, like many other businessmen of the time, I conducted a good deal of my business on the golf course. It was there that I met a close friend, a man whom I later helped to build a cottage in Muskoka, in the district known as Hudson Point. My assistance to him was rewarded by his offering me access to his cottage. It was in this area of Muskoka that we built a cottage — Barlochan was just across the water — a cottage we have enjoyed as a family for over fifty years.

Lumber for the cottages was brought in by barge from the lumberyard. Other supplies would be carted by rail and by car to Gravenhurst, picked up with the passengers and carried by boat to various cottage sites. I remember that, during our building period, a boatload of supplies from Aikenhead's sank under its own weight. Everything, even our boat and motor, had to be carefully dried by hand. Aikenhead's Hardware Store on Temperance Street was the largest hardware store in Toronto and was owned by the family whom we had known in Lorne Park. To build our cottage, I used vertical plank siding, one inch by ten inches wide, made of white undressed pine. It cost me eighteen dollars per thousand at the time of purchase. Today, it can't be purchased at any price!

As cottagers, we would work in the city until noon Saturday, spend all day Sunday building and supervising carpenters at work on our cottage, enjoy all day Monday in the cottage and then return for work in Toronto on Tuesday morning. Though the opposition to working on Sunday had been relaxed by then, we would still conscientiously attend church every Sunday morning as a family. This kind of weekend was a common business and social practice for the hundreds of Torontonians who had cottages in Muskoka.

The shortened work week enacted by the government during the war, the improved highways and the increased prosperity which prevailed in the city after the war, all contributed to making this way of life more common in the muggy summers. More people could afford to purchase property and build cottages. It was no longer limited to the rich as it had been during our Lorne Park and Mimico Beach days.

In time, roads were built into our property. Prior to that, like hundreds of other cottagers, we had obtained our supplies from a boat run by the Mills family from Milford Bay. They ran an excellent supply boat stocked with food, candles and all sorts of other necessities. If your wharf was in good condition they would tie up there. If not, they would toot their whistle, drop anchor just out from your property and you would take your boat out to them to get your supplies. It was a pleasant way to shop without crowds!

In our early days there was no electricity in Muskoka, nor were there any waterworks. I can remember hooking up a radio to a large wet battery used for cars. In fact, we used three different batteries of three different sizes for the various tasks. Our radio was an Atwater-Kent Radio, about two feet in height. We ran a wire along the verandah of the cottage and down to the trees at the water's edge on which we used a lightning arrester to prevent fire. Because of the lack of interference, we were able to pick up over forty stations. Sitting in the Muskoka silence on our verandah, listening to the radio was an enormously exciting phenomena.

This was a time of telecommunications discovery. As a young teacher in Sunday School, I can remember going to a friend's house and listening to a flautist broadcasting from New York. It seemed magical, as the music wafted out of the air in 1920. My friend had used "peanut tubes" and wire as an antenna to catch the radio waves.

By the time we had built our cottage in Muskoka and had lived through the Second World War, radio was an accepted medium of communication, something we turned to for regular news and weather reports. The old sense of awe when we tuned in was gone. The nineteen-fifties brought us television. The wonders of electronic evolution were magnificent, and soon, as most of the others who experienced it, we were quick to purchase and enjoy television.

Ours was a typical Toronto life after the Second World War. By 1950 the population of the city was over one million people. The Yonge Street subway had been begun; new roads were being completed in the city, as were roads toward the city. The Queen Elizabeth Highway was completed. Because of the tremendous production of electricity from the Niagara Falls Power Station, there seemed to be an abundance of power to burn, so it was decided to illuminate the Queen Elizabeth, the first four-lane highway in the world to be illuminated.

There were improved social services in Toronto and an acceptance of the need for these services. There was a great optimism for the future and more building was being undertaken in the city. It became legal to drink in hotels although, High Park, once the Howard Park district, remained opposed to the concept and has remained dry until the present day. When the idea was accepted by the majority of

Toronto and the rest of Ontario's population, High Park residents defeated George Drew, their member in Queen's Park and the Premier of the province, the man who had sponsored the bill.

In April 1953, Bill 80 created Metropolitan Toronto, a marriage of the City of Toronto and its twelve suburban neighbours. Each district elected its own mayor or reeve to sit on the council and in addition the City of Toronto contributed twelve representative councillors including her Mayor. In total, twenty-five representatives sat on the original Metropolitan Toronto Council. This board then elected a Metro Chairman to oversee development of public works such as the construction of highways, sewers and waterworks and the provision of other civic services. Initially the council concentrated on the provision of essential physical services and there was a boom in this type of construction. Frederick G. Gardiner, who became known as "Big Daddy" Gardiner, and his council were sworn into office in 1953 and Gardiner became the first Chairman of Metropolitan Toronto. The first new public works project completed under his chairmanship was the construction of a water main feeding to North York, a borough which had always had difficulty with its water supply.

This was the first successful two-tiered metro-politan government in North America and many politicians from the US and across Canada came to see how it worked. The cooperation and resulting greater savings facilitated by this government made services more efficient and cheaper.

Big Daddy Gardiner was keen on development and saw many of his ambitious projects completed during his many years in office including the Gardiner Expressway, which today bears his name as a permanent reminder of this dynamic man's impact on the growing city. The Don Valley Parkway, second subway (the Bloor Street line) and the new City Hall were also begun during this period of optimism, expansion and growth. Population of the city was increasing at a rate of around fifty thousand people a year.

The St. Lawrence Seaway construction was finally approved and begun. The Toronto Transit Commission replaced the Toronto Transportation Commission, forming a monopoly except for trains and taxis in a two-hundred-and-forty square-mile area. Many extra miles of track were built to connect the suburbs and the inner core of the city. The streetcars became known as the "red rattlers". The fare was raised for the first time since the formation of the TTC from four tickets for a quarter to three tickets for a quarter. In March 1954 the subway line, Canada's first, was opened on Yonge Street, running from Eglinton to Union Station. It was integrated with bus and streetcar lines already operating in the city. Service was maintained from six in the morning until one-thirty in the morning. It rapidly became popular and, in 1972, the TTC recorded the highest per capita utilization of any public transit system in North America. Since the first soil was dug for the Toronto subway system, it has been continuously upgraded, expanded and improved.

The Kiwanis were always looking for ways to help the young kids of Toronto and we were active in the fifties. We devised the idea of an annual treasure hunt organized in High Park. The idea was that we would drop milk bottle caps all through the park and that the kid who found the specially marked one would be given a bicycle. There were other prizes, but this was the grand one. Soon, the kids caught onto the system and began to follow us into the bushes when we were making random drops through holes in our pockets. When they did this, of course, the competition became unfair and we had to change the system.

I thought that we should drop the caps into the park from an airplane. Because it was my idea, I was given the job of finding the appropriate airplane for the task. I contacted a client of mine who was a pilot with a small airline and he was given a plane free of charge to take me up over the park. I remember clearly, sitting in the open cockpit, with my bag full of milk caps. We had obtained permission from the city to fly at four hundred feet, over sixteen hundred feet below the level at which planes generally fly over the city. The annual treasure hunt was a big event in an optimistic city. Every kid involved, and there would be about five thousand of them, would be given an apple delivered in the huge tractor trailers of National Grocers. There would be bags of candy and plenty of other prizes. Many city firms donated them to us. Many Toronto children of the time rode bicycles won in the Kiwanis Annual High Park Treasure Hunt.

During all this time of change in the city, the Humber River flowed quietly south through Weston and Toronto to Lake Ontario with many small creeks and streams flowing into it. This was the way it had been over the years, perhaps centuries. Hundreds of roads crossed it back and forth. The odd bridge would sometimes be damaged or perhaps even washed out in the annual run-off or by a particularly heavy thunderstorm, but repairs were promptly made and forgotten.

I spent twenty-five years living along the Humber River and I still remember the sounds like thunder as the ice broke up in the spring. Sometimes ice jams had to be manually broken up, even dynamited, because blockage of the melting ice would create huge flooded areas of water. Nonetheless, every spring the stone bridge on the Humber at the Old Mill would be lined with fishermen standing shoulder to shoulder, pole to pole. The sucker or catfish, so common in those waters, provided many tasty meals. Its rich flesh was a much-enjoyed gourmet treat.

In October 1954 the Humber was slightly swollen by rain but peaceful. This wasn't an unusual condition. Hurricanes had been reported forming in the Caribbean Sea and in the Gulf of Mexico this year as they had been many times before during this season. It wasn't unusual. We expected to hear about them pounding the shorelines mercilessly down on the Gulf, but they remained a problem "down there" and not personally connected to us, unless our church established a fund to assist victims of an area badly hit by a storm. Generally, the storms disappeared inland dissipating gradually. There was often much destruction of life and property in the wake of their violence before they played themselves out. Still, they had little or no impact on Torontonians.

The storm causing most of the chaos that October was Hurricane Hazel. She had circled around the Caribbean and then decided to come north travelling up the Atlantic coast. Her course was unusual, but still Toronto was unconcerned by her progress.

We had planned and built our last home on the high banks overlooking the Humber. Our lot was over three hundred and seventy feet deep with a fine creek, named Silver Creek, at the rear of our lot. We had set our two-storey house eighty feet from the street, at the edge of the escarpment. We could walk out of the lower floor of the house directly onto the back lawn.

Our last child was married at Kingsway Lambton United Church on October 8, 1954, and a sixty-foot marquise tent had been set up on the lower lawn for the reception. It had been a wonderful day for everybody. Little did we know it then, but we were very lucky. Seven days later, "Hazel" was in our backyard.

We had watched the actions of the hurricane on the television and feared nothing, thinking it would do what all the other hurricanes before it had done — blow itself out over land or sea. We had two days of steady east winds and rain. On the Friday afternoon, it started to rain hard and, by ten in the evening, it was still pelting down in a steady stream. Sheets of water seemed to connect the earth and the sky. The trees were bending down so low, you feared that they would break; and then the wind started to roar. The neighbours on either side of us came out to see what was going on, but, although we were all alarmed, there was nothing we could do. Then the power went off and so did the phone connections. Transistor radio reports kept us informed of our position. The hurricane had us in her grip.

One of our family lived in Don Mills but we could not contact him. Instead, we waited it out and worried.

There were reports that some of the main roads were closed because of the possibility of bridge washouts. It was a fearful night. Our daughter and her new husband got the ship report on the storm stating that the Humber was washing over its banks and that all of Etobicoke was in the middle of the storm. They tried to get word through to us, but all efforts failed. Hundreds of families panicked, unable to get word on who was in trouble and who was safely away from the storm.

When daylight came in the morning, I looked out our windows on to what had been a river less than one hundred feet wide to a lake over half a mile wide on the flooded portions of the Lambton Golf Fairways. Tops of bushes and trees poked their heads through the surface of the lake. This was only the beginning.

In the southward sweep of the river, its long graceful bends in several places had left flat land, high above any previously recorded watermark. As the city had grown, this land had become useful for building lots. Sewers, drains and waterworks had been put in and brick houses built on the serviced lots. Nobody ever dreamed they would be unsafe, but it was on these homes plus hundreds of square miles of farmland and villages that Hurricane Hazel had chosen to empty her clouds. The natural watershed flowed toward the Humber River and as the rain continued unabated, the creeks had soon overflowed; the further down river you were the worse the accumulation of water. The swollen Humber River had swept down on unsuspecting, sleeping people, her waves of water becoming higher and higher, stronger and stronger, as they progressed southward. Houses on the low lands were washed away. People were washed away trying to salvage their possessions. I did not know it, but my son, John, had been down on the riverbank helping to try to save a man who was hanging on to a tree trunk. Some of the volunteer firemen were putting a ladder out to the man. They managed to get him off the tree, but only moments later, with my son safe on higher ground, an enormous ten-foot wave of water came down the river and washed away the fire truck and the men into the torrent. Although the truck was later recovered, five of the men were lost.

When it was all totalled up, there were over eighty-one lives lost and many millions of dollars of property destroyed. It had been a terrible night for Etobicoke families; and for all of Toronto. The Humber Valley had suffered the greatest devastation and loss of life, but the Don River Valley had also been struck severely by the disaster.

A twisted iron railing on the top of the Scarlett Road Bridge, ten feet above the riverbed, remained as a stunning memorial of the heights the river had reached that night, and of the destruction it had wrought. Although we had been frightened and uncomfortable, not knowing what had happened to our son and his family nor he about us, we had been luckier than many families.

No Civil Defence Unit had been organized to provide the essential coordinated help when the Highland Creek, the Don and Humber Rivers, the Etobicoke and Sixteen-Mile creeks and even the Credit River had overflowed that night. Individuals and volunteers performed hundreds of acts of courage. The Salvation Army and many other volunteer and paid agencies immediately organized relief.

Hydro worked non-stop to restore power; telephone lines were installed or repaired to re-establish communication. Huge donations came from all over Canada and as far away as England to assist in the disaster fund created to help the families who had lost their homes and all of their possessions. Local township, city and provincial governments immediately set up commissions to survey, explore and acquire complete authority to prevent such a tragedy from recurring.

In 1958 the Metro Conservation Authority was established under the directorship of Dr. G. Ross Lord with a mandate to coordinate the establishment of an early flood warning system, to purchase lands which were vulnerable to flooding, to build dams and reservoirs to help prevent flooding and to organize reforestation. The agency had jurisdiction over one thousand square miles to work toward flood control and water conservation, recognizing that valleys are natural floodways.

Future emergencies, if and when they occur, will be dealt with by the agency since established to coordinate such an effort. The Chief of Police has developed a coordinated plan and been empowered to organize the efforts should it ever become necessary.

The effectiveness of Metro Toronto as a political governing entity has encouraged many local conservation authorities to form regional government bodies providing a more cohesive municipal approach.

Postscript

By the mid-fifties the automobile and a massive migration to Toronto had caused the development of suburban housing tracts and shopping malls further and further away from the core of the city. Eaton's and Simpsons, once single, downtown department stores, now frequently have major branches in these shopping complexes. Chain stores such as Loblaws are also part of these complexes. The stores have become larger and more modern, concentrating on high sales volumes in order to make a profit. These food stores now act as umbrellas for various special services such as bakeries, delicatessens, and other food operations. It is a far cry from the door-to-door pedlars from whom my family and most of Toronto bought the majority of their supplies when I was a boy. Simpsons at Queen and Yonge, a store built soon after I was born, has been declared an historic Toronto building.

Today, the City of Toronto is a very different place from the city in which I shared my life with many of her former hard-working, great citizens. She is larger and growing larger daily. The city's elbow room is gone and individualism is disappearing. Things are streamlined for efficiency and much gracious living has disappeared. Much of Toronto's citizenry is in a constant hurry — getting from one place to another without being anywhere in between. Nonetheless, it is the city's good men and women who make Toronto the important and beautiful city that she is today.

Bibliography

Books

Arthur, Eric. *Toronto No Mean City.* Toronto:
University of Toronto Press, Second Edition, 1974.

Barry, James P. *The Fate of the Lakes, A Portrait of
the Great Lakes.* Toronto: G.R. Welch Company,
Copyright 1972 by Baker Book House Company.

Bromley, John F. and Jack May. *Fifty Years of
Progressive Transit.* Toronto: Electric Railroaders
Assocation, 1973.

Colton, Timothy J. *Big Daddy: Frederick G. Gardiner
and the Building of Metropolitan Toronto.*
Toronto: University of Toronto Press, 1980.

Filey, Mike, *Toronto, City Life: Old and New,*
Toronto: Foster and Scott, General Publishing
Company, 1979.

French, William. *A Most Unlikely Village.* Toronto:
Ryerson Press, 1964

Glazebrook. G.P. de T. *The Story of Toronto.*
Toronto: University of Toronto Press, 1971.

Guillet, Edwin C. *Toronto from Trading Post to
Great City.* Toronto: The Ontario Publishing
Company, 1934.

Hathaway, E.J. *The Story of the Old Fort at Toronto.*
Toronto: The Macmillan Company of Canada Ltd.
at St. Martin's House, 1934.

Jameson, Anne Brownell. *Winter Studies and
Summer Rambles in Canada,* edited by James J.
Talman and Elsie McLeod Murray. Toronto:
Thomas Nelson and Sons, 1943.

Kennedy, Betty. *Hurricane Hazel.* Toronto:
Macmillan of Canada, 1979.

Kenyon, Roy, *The Golden Years of Trucking.*
Toronto: Ontario Trucking Association, Webcom,
1977.

Lane, Grace. *Brief Halt at Mile "50".* Toronto:
The United Church Publishing House, 1974.

Langston, Anne. *A Gentlewoman in Upper Canada:
The Journals of Anne Langston,* edited by H.H.
Langston. Toronto: Clarke, Irwin and Company
Ltd., 1950.

Masters, Donald C. *The Rise of Toronto, 1850-90.*
Toronto: University of Toronto Press, 1947.

Middleton, Jesse Edgar. *The Municipality of Toronto:
A History.* Toronto and New York: The Dominion
Publishing Company, 1923. Vol. 1, chapter 2,
"The Toronto Harbour" by E.V. Roberts.

Moyles, R.G. *The Blood and Fire in Canada.* Toronto:
Peter Martin Associates, 1977.

Myers, Jan. *The Great Canadian Road,* Toronto: Red
Rock Publishing Company Ltd., 1977.

Paris, Erna. *Jews: An Account of Their Experience in
Canada.* Toronto: Macmillan of Canada, 1979.

Scadding, Henry. *Toronto of Old,* Abridged and
edited by F.H. Armstrong. Toronto: Oxford
University Press, 1960.

Schull, Joseph. *Ontario Since 1867.* Toronto:
McCelland and Stewart, 1978.

Thompson, Austin Seton. *Spadina: A Story of Old
Toronto.* Toronto: Pagurian Press Ltd., 1975.

Additional Pamphlets, articles and interviews

*A Responsive Chord: The Story of Toronto
Mendelssohn Choir,* 1894-1969, Toronto.

Toronto the Green, published by the Toronto Field
Naturalists' Club, Toronto, 1976.

The Toronto Fire Department Report: *Report on the
S.S. Noronic Holocaust,* September 17, 1949.

Conservation, 1977-82. The Metropolitan Toronto and Region Conservation Authority, a series of booklets.

Port of Toronto News, series of articles starting in May 1973, ending August-September 1974.

Loblaw's History, a short piece prepared and released by the George Weston Ltd. Public Relations Department.

Insurers' Advisory Organization of Canada. Vol, 17, no. 3, 1981.

Historical notes prepared by Church of St. Stephen-in-the-Fields, College Street and Bellevue Avenue, Toronto, E.G. Moogk, September 1976.

Board of Trade Journal, October 1971, ''Toronto Fire-fighting: Past and Present,'' Charles R. Chambers, Fire Chief Toronto Fire Department; plus assorted journals from the Chamber of Commerce library.

Interviews with: Colonel Hurt of the Royal Canadian Military Institute: Miss Elizabeth M.Geraghty, Bell Canada historian in Montreal; George M. Parke, Ontario Trucking Association; Lillian Purcell, St. Stephen-in-the-Field, secretary, and others.

City of Toronto Archives and City Council records.

Index